ASSESSMENT AS LEARNING

EXPERTS IN ASSESSMENT™

SERIES EDITORS
THOMAS R. GUSKEY AND ROBERT J. MARZANO

Please call our toll-free number (800–818–7243)
or visit our website (www.corwinpress.com)
to order individual titles or the entire series.

ASSESSMENT AS LEARNING

USING CLASSROOM ASSESSMENT
TO MAXIMIZE STUDENT LEARNING

LORNA M. EARL

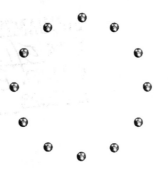

EXPERTS IN ASSESSMENT™

SERIES EDITORS
THOMAS R. GUSKEY AND ROBERT J. MARZANO

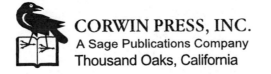

CORWIN PRESS, INC.
A Sage Publications Company
Thousand Oaks, California

For information:

Corwin Press, Inc.
A Sage Publications Company
2455 Teller Road
Thousand Oaks, California 91320
www.corwinpress.com

Sage Publications Ltd.
6 Bonhill Street
London EC2A 4PU
United Kingdom

Sage Publications India Pvt. Ltd.
B-42, Panchsheel Enclave
Post Box 4109
New Delhi 110 017 India

Printed in the United States of America

Library of Congress Cataloging-in-Publication Data

Earl, Lorna M. (Lorna Maxine), 1948-
Assessment as learning: Using classroom assessment to maximize
student learning / Lorna M. Earl.
     p. cm. — (Experts in assessment series)
Includes bibliographical references and index.
ISBN 0-7619-4625-X (cloth) — ISBN 0-7619-4626-8 (pbk.)
   1. Educational tests and measurements. 2. Learning. I. Title.
II. Experts in assessment.
LB3051.E19 2003
371.26′4—dc21

                                                    2003002364

03   04   05   06   10   9   8   7   6   5   4   3   2   1

Acquisitions Editor:	Rachel Livsey
Editorial Assistant:	Phyllis Cappello
Production Editor:	Melanie Birdsall
Copy Editor:	Liann Lech
Typesetter:	C&M Digitals (P) Ltd.
Proofreader:	Teresa Herlinger
Indexer:	Kathy Paparchontis
Cover Designer:	Tracy E. Miller

Contents

Series Editors' Introduction

Standards, assessment, accountability, and grading—these are the issues that dominated discussions of education in the 1990s. Today, they are at the center of every modern education reform effort. As educators turn to the task of implementing these reforms, they face a complex array of questions and concerns that little in their background or previous experience has prepared them to address. This series is designed to help in that challenging task.

In selecting the authors, we went to individuals recognized as true experts in the field. The ideas of these scholar-practitioners have already helped shape current discussions of standards, assessment, accountability, and grading. But equally important, their work reflects a deep understanding of the complexities involved in implementation. As they developed their books for this series, we asked them to extend their thinking, push the edge, and present new perspectives on what should be done and how to do it. That is precisely what they did. The books they crafted provide not only cutting-edge perspectives but also practical guidelines for successful implementation.

We have several goals for this series. First, that it be used by teachers, school leaders, policymakers, government officials, and all those concerned with these crucial aspects of education reform. Second, that it helps broaden understanding of the complex issues involved in standards, assessment, accountability, and grading. Third, that it leads to more thoughtful policies and programs. Fourth, and most important, that it helps accomplish the basic goal for which all reform initiatives are intended—namely, to enable all students to learn excellently and to gain the many positive benefits of that success.

Thomas R. Guskey
Robert J. Marzano
Series Editors

Preface

Why This Book?

For almost 30 years, I have been working with teachers and administrators in schools and districts in the province of Ontario, Canada, as a colleague, researcher, and "critical friend." My work has taken me into classrooms and staff rooms, marking sessions and student-led conferences, professional development sessions and teacher discussion groups.

From my unique vantage point of researcher, observer, and colleague in many classrooms, I was struck by the way assessment always came at the end, not only in the unit of work but also in teachers' planning. And even in the planning, assessment received little attention. After columns of objectives and teaching strategies and resources in the planning grid, the assessment column would sit ominously stark, with cryptic entries such as "test" or "worksheet" or "project." Assessment was almost an afterthought. At the same time, it often seemed as though too much time was being dedicated to testing that didn't go anywhere.

I routinely heard that "assessment is the hardest part." As a young researcher working in a school district, I was intrigued by the tensions and challenges that assessment created for teachers. I became a student of the ways and means of classroom assessment, sometimes informally, sometimes more formally. Although the recent preoccupation with assessment as a lever for educational reform has brought the discussion to the foreground, teachers have always expressed concern about their roles as assessors. In some recent research, middle years teachers told us that they are being caught between competing purposes of classroom assessment and are often confused and frustrated by the difficulties that they experience as they try to reconcile the demands (Hargreaves, Earl, Moore, & Manning, 2001).

Who Is This Book For?

I have written this book for those teachers and school leaders who are struggling with and trying to come to grips with the conflict that they feel in relation to assessment. I hope that it will provide some alternate perspectives and beliefs about the role that assessment can play in the daily working of schools and classrooms, with real examples of how teachers are making assessment work to enhance student learning.

Teachers and school leaders can use this book as a focus for their discussions about what assessment means, especially as a part of learning and as a stimulus for deciding how they might change their practices. But changing practices will not be enough. An important element of these discussions and reflections should be the role of schooling and the role of educators in schools. Why? Because embedding some of the changes into routine practices without this discussion is unlikely to have much influence. Assessment as learning is premised on assumptions and beliefs that are simple in their articulation and very difficult in their application. Throughout the book, I have highlighted these assumptions by placing them in boxes. I invite you to consider your personal assumptions as you read mine and think about how your beliefs contribute to the way you engage in your work as a teacher.

I have also included examples from my own experience and the experience of colleagues, preservice candidates, and graduate students with whom I have worked throughout the book. These are all identified as "The Case of. . . ." I find them all compelling and exciting images of the challenges and the possibilities that exist for making assessment work for students. I hope you do, too. Here is the first one.

"The Case of Understanding Mathematics Learning and Assessment"

I have had the pleasure, over several years, of working with a wonderful young secondary mathematics teacher who came to me because of an interest in learning more about assessment. During our association, she has given me insights into the difficulties associated with changing deeply held beliefs that are based on a lifetime of personal experience. At one point, she came to me with a new understanding on her part. "I know how to teach calculus," she said. "I just don't know what to do when they don't get it." After her own time in school, always successful and delighting in the intellectual challenge that mathematics provided, she had had a major epiphany. Her experience was not the same as the experience of her students, and she did not know what they were encountering when calculus was not "obvious" to them, as it was to her. Helping them learn meant finding out what concepts, misconceptions, skills, and relationships make up "getting calculus" so that she could help them unpack their own learning.

After being part of several graduate courses about classroom assessment and attending a range of workshops and conferences dedicated to the topic, this same teacher read the draft manuscript for this book. Another epiphany: "I've heard lots of people talk about ideas like connecting assessment to learning, giving feedback, encouraging students to talk about their thinking, but you know what? I didn't get it. I kept saying to myself, 'I do that.' And I do, but not for the same reasons. At the end of the day, I still focused on what the information told me about how to give them a grade. Their learning was secondary."

Taken together, these realizations on her part not only are dramatic shifts in her thinking that are resulting in some serious changes to her practice and even her knowledge about the underpinnings of her subject area, but they also demonstrate how subtle and challenging making these changes can be. It seems so easy, even commonplace, to change the language and not the concepts, to believe that the work is done, when it has barely started.

What Is This Book About?

This book is about classroom assessment—the kind of assessment that happens every day in classrooms everywhere. Certainly, there are other kinds of assessment in education, and much has and will be written about them, but not in this book. Instead, the focus is on what teachers and students do, what they *can* do, how they think, and how they might think about routine classroom assessment as an inextricable part of learning. The ideas in this book arise out of my musings, observations, and conversations with students and teachers; from hours of reading material; and from discussions with people around the world who are struggling with the same issues. Consequently, this book is premised on a number of beliefs and assumptions about the nature and purpose of schooling and the role of teaching and assessment in the learning process. The major and most dramatic assumption is that assessment can and should be much more than a check on learning that comes at the end. It is an integral part of the learning process that, all too often, has been ignored. Historically, educational assessment has largely been assessment *of* learning, designed to accredit or judge the work of students. Sometimes, it has been assessment *for* learning, with feedback loops to ensure that students are given cues to review their learning and move forward. Assessment *as* learning goes even deeper, however, and draws on the role of personal monitoring and challenging of ideas that are embedded in the learning process, and the role of both students and teachers in fostering this process. *Assessment As Learning* is not superficial tampering. It is a fundamental shift in thinking about teaching and assessment, and about the relationship between them.

Throughout the book, my assumptions and perspectives will become clearer. When they do, I will attempt to provide a rationale and support for choosing this route as a compelling one for moving toward the kind of schooling that I believe will serve us all well. To that end, I have tried to shed some light on the assessment dilemmas that teachers feel, provide some insights into the complexity behind these tensions, and offer some suggestions for consideration in classrooms. I have not provided detailed directions for implementing classroom assessment strategies. Instead, I have tried to offer the following:

• An understanding of the reasons behind the confusion and discomfort that surround classroom assessment by detailing the way that the changing role of schooling and our increasing knowledge about the nature of learning have made classroom assessment much more complex

• Insight into the powerful influence that classroom assessment can have on students' learning

• Examples of mechanisms for effective use of assessment as learning in a variety of contexts, many of them drawn from actual examples provided by teachers whom I have come to know through my work

Organization of This Book

The book is organized into 11 chapters. Chapter 1 sets the stage for considering a new view of learning and assessment that argues for connecting them as part of the same process. Chapter 2 is a brief history of assessment, with attention to the influence of the current large-scale reform movement on classroom assessment. In Chapter 3, I make the case for considering assessment *of* learning, *for* learning, and *as* learning and make a concerted effort to rationalize shifting the existing balance among them in schools. Following the discussion of the purposes of assessment in relation to learning, Chapter 4 is about learning as the primary purpose for schools, and Chapter 5 details the links that exist between learning and assessment.

The next five chapters revisit what we know about learning and consider how assessment can contribute to deeper and better learning for students. Chapter 6 addresses diagnostic assessment—finding out what students believe to be true. The focus in Chapter 7 is motivation and the role that assessment can play in motivating students. In

Chapters 8 and 9, I get to the heart of the matter: How can assessment enhance and extend learning? Chapter 10 addresses the essential role of reflection and self-assessment in learning.

Finally, in Chapter 11, I have tried to identify some of the specific demands that looking at assessment as learning will make on teachers and to offer glimpses of what teachers should think about as they work to get to assessment that maximizes learning for all students.

At the end of each chapter, I have included some "Ideas for Follow-Up" that might be useful as groups of educators read and think about assessment as learning together. The questions are not comprehensive, but perhaps they can offer a starting point for conversation and sharing.

Writing this book has been a powerful learning experience for me. I have been forced to clarify my own thinking, challenge my assumptions, and put my ideas forward for constructive criticism from my colleagues and mentors, from my students and their students. I now find myself in the space between the production and the feedback. All comments are welcome. I hope this volume helps to stimulate conversation and challenge ideas—my own as well as others'.

Acknowledgments

First and foremost, thank you to all of the teachers, students, and colleagues who have challenged my thinking and pushed me to make classroom assessment my passion. In particular, thanks to Karen Allin, Rich Cornwall, Mary Lou McKinley, Rick Parsons, and Nancy Torrance, who provided assistance, insight, and wonderful examples of classroom assessment as learning, and to Louise Stoll, Karen Allin, Michele Schmidt, and Steven Katz for being, as always, my "critical friends."

Many teachers have known, in their hearts, about the role that classroom assessment plays in learning. To all of the researchers who continue to examine and describe the power of classroom assessment, you have given them the evidence that they need to continue with the struggle to make learning the raison d'etre of schools. From these teachers and the others who follow—thank you.

My own journey of awareness about the potential for classroom assessment as a vehicle for learning came from a lucky encounter (and subsequent long friendship) with Rick Stiggins, who had the courage to say, "I believe in teachers, I believe in classroom assessment, and I'll stake my career on it." We are all so grateful that he did and still does speak out with integrity, passion, and truth. Closer to home is my mentor and good friend, Bob Wilson, who pushes, cajoles, and never ceases to remind me that teachers are at the heart of learning in schools, and that they often do know best, even when they don't have the language to articulate their knowing. He inspires me to listen, and listen, and listen.

Once I was hooked on assessment, I have had the privilege to work with some wonderful and insightful colleagues and graduate students who constantly push me and teach me. To all of you in Scarborough, at OISE/UT, and around the world, thank you.

Finally, to family and friends who have listened to my ranting and watched me avoid writing in every possible way. You know what you have contributed—from a place at the table on Arran Lake to write, to answering midnight phone calls with a request for a virtual hug. I love you all.

About the Author

Lorna Earl, Ph.D., is Associate Professor in the Theory and Policy Studies Department at the Ontario Institute for Studies in Education at the University of Toronto and Head of the OISE/UT International Centre for Educational Change. Her experience as a Research Director in a large school district and as the first Director of Assessment for the Ontario provincial Education Quality and Accountability Office, when it was formed in 1995, have kept her immersed in the study of assessment in schools for almost 30 years. Her work in Canada, England, the United States, Australia, and New Zealand, and her interest in the international applications of assessment ideas, have given her experience in many contexts. This allows her to see similarities and differences that emerge as educators and governments struggle with the challenges that face schools in many locales.

CHAPTER 1

The Evolution of Assessment

Educational reform in the past decade has felt like a roller coaster ride for most teachers and schools. Schools reflect the changes that are occurring more broadly in society, and there seems to be no end to the changes (economic, cultural, political, and socioeconomic) that schools are expected to keep up with, or even lead. As Hargreaves (1994) reminds us, "Few people want to do much about the economy, but everyone—politicians, the media, and the public alike—wants to do something about education" (p. 17). The role of education is hotly debated in boardrooms, living rooms, and staff rooms.

Teachers and administrators are caught in the middle of what often appear to be conflicting and countervailing demands, struggling to maintain their balance. They are expected to navigate their passage through the unrest and uncertainty about how schools should be organized, what should be taught, how it should be taught, and how assessment should occur. At the same time, they are expected to continue to exert their professional influence by staying abreast of advances in understanding of human learning and of effective schools. The prospects are daunting, but the possibilities are compelling.

For a long time, extended education was available only to a small elite group. Schools were designed to provide the minimum education required for employment and engagement in the broader culture. For most students, this meant attending school long enough to learn the 3Rs and get a minimal understanding of the society in which they lived. Only a few students continued on to secondary school and beyond. Over time, as societies have changed, schools have evolved progressively from serving this elite group, to working with the larger numbers and wider aspirations of a middle class, to dealing with the responsibility for educating all young people.

For most of the 20th century, the conception of learning was a behaviorist one that focused on learning specific, discrete skills and facts in a hierarchical sequence. Schools were charged with their transmission to students. Over time, these theories have been challenged by a social constructivist view of learning that emphasizes learning as a cognitive process that is shaped by prior knowledge and cultural perspectives. Teachers are expected to attend both to the demands of a fixed school curriculum generated by cultural/societal demands and to the needs of individual children with varied understandings, backgrounds, and interests who make up a class. They are caught between an awareness that young people construct their own view of the world through ideas that have some meaning for them and the expectations of the social milieu in which they live (Katz, Earl, & Olsen, 2001).

Traditionally, assessment and tests or examinations were synonymous, and their role was clear and consistent with the purposes of schooling—testing of segmented competencies and knowledge from the school curriculum as a way of sorting students into groups and deciding about future schooling. Assessment was based on the "concordance" or "fidelity" of the students' responses to the material that was delivered. As we come to know more about how learning happens, assessment takes on a different sheen. In our work, we have found that teachers are uneasy about having a single purpose for assessment. They are increasingly aware that assessment has multiple purposes and that they need a toolbox full of assessment ideas to address them all.

"The Case of Standards-Based Assessment"

In our book, *Learning to Change,* Andy Hargreaves and I wrote about how middle school teachers were responding to mandated changes in curriculum and assessment. In this longitudinal study, we followed 29 teachers from four different school districts who were actively engaged in efforts to incorporate the changes into their practices. When it came to assessment, they were confused, frustrated, and anxious. They told us that assessment was the hardest part of their work and gave us vivid examples of the inconsistencies and contradictions that they were facing.

We are having trouble because the marks don't mesh with the standards-based report card. I don't know how to relate them.

We're supposed to be teaching to the standards and helping kids learn how to learn. But then they have the large-scale tests. What does the curriculum have to do with common testing?

What about the students who don't get it? There is so much in the curriculum, I can't stop and work with them but that's my job, isn't it?

The high school mathematics department would like to issue a standardized test to all the incoming students. It makes me think about what I've been doing all year. I send the kids to them with detailed reports based on the standards. I talk about integers and decimals and geometry. What are they going to do with those reports?

These teachers were struggling with the paradox of classroom assessment. It does have multiple purposes. As Wilson (1996) describes it, assessment must satisfy many goals, such as providing feedback to students, offering diagnostic information for the teacher to use, providing summary information for record keeping, proffering evidence for reports, and directing efforts at curriculum and instructional adaptations. There is no single activity called "classroom assessment," and inherent tensions exist among the different purposes that are not trivial. Contradictions in classroom assessment processes are unavoidable. The challenge that these teachers were facing was how to untangle the issues that are embedded in these tensions and formulate plans that honor the complexity of the assessment process, in ways that made sense to them.

Defining the Future

Navigating these troubled waters requires more than tinkering with practice. It means that teachers and administrators are having to rethink their beliefs about issues as lofty as "What are schools for?" "Whom do schools serve?" and "What is our professional role in creating the schools we need?"

Hedley Beare (2001), an Australian researcher, identified the following three categories of futures for education and for societies as a whole:

- *Possible futures*—things that could happen, although many of them are unlikely

- *Probable futures*—things that probably will happen, unless something is done to turn events around

- *Preferred futures*—things that you prefer to have happen and/or that you would like to happen

He also issued a challenge to educators everywhere when he stated that it is possible to take deliberate actions to maximize the chance of achieving preferred futures—for young people, for the teaching profession, for schools, and for societies. We each need to take the time to decide what it is that we believe education is for and what role assessment should play: not because someone tells us, or the rules dictate, but because we believe it is right and just. Once we have an image of the future we prefer, getting there is possible. It may be difficult; we may have to change, to learn, to live in dissonance, and to stand firm in our beliefs. But it is possible.

My preferred future is a world in which young people not only possess competence and confidence in a broad range of areas, but also the tools to adapt to new knowledge as it comes along, and the dispositions to function wisely and with civility in a fast-paced and unpredictable world. I also have an image of how assessment fits in this preferred future. I described it first in an earlier book about classroom assessment (Earl & Cousins, 1995) as follows:

> I can imagine a day, in the not too distant future, when assessment and evaluation are not viewed with foreboding and terror; not separated from teaching and learning; not used to punish or prohibit access to important learning; and not seen as private, mystical ceremonies. Instead, assessment and teaching/learning will be reciprocal, each contributing to the other in ways that enhance both. Assessment will reveal not only what students know and understand, but will also capture how those new learnings came about and will provide a range in variety and quality of work that show the depth, breadth and growth of each student's thinking. This wealth of information will, in its turn, be used to provoke further learning and focused instruction. (p. 57)

In the rest of this volume, I offer ideas, suggestions, and images to illustrate the potential of realizing this preferred future.

Ideas for Follow-Up

1.   How comfortable are you with your current approach to classroom assessment? What questions do you have about what you are doing?

2.   What is your preferred future for education and for assessment? What is the probable future, given how things are now?

Rethinking Assessment

A lthough assessment is a relatively new word in education, the process of gathering information about student performance and using it in schools has had a long and contentious history. One way of understanding assessment better is to situate it in the social, economic, and political context of the times.

A Brief History of Assessment

Formal and informal assessment of learning has existed for centuries—from the early Chinese civil service exams for entry into high public office, to public presentations by students of Aristotle, to practical assessments for entrance to craft guilds. It wasn't until industrialization and universal schooling at the turn of the past century, however, that schools became significant social institutions and evaluation of student achievement, as we know it, became a significant dimension of schooling. For centuries, the young in a community followed traditional occupations for which they learned "on the job," and schooling was a luxury. With the industrial revolution, people moved from rural to urban communities, and large numbers of newcomers emigrated from many countries and cultures. This led to larger organizations and a need to absorb and educate many young people in urban centers with a different social structure and economic base. The notion of universal education was born.

For most of the 20th century, and even now, factories have dominated the economy, and schools organized around a factory model have been consistent with the world around them. Kindergarten-sized units of raw material are put onto the first bench of the "plant" and

Learning by direct sharing in the pursuits of grown-ups becomes increasingly difficult except in the case of the less advanced occupations. Much of what adults do is so remote in space and in meaning that playful imitation is less and less adequate to reproduce its spirit. Ability to share effectively in adult activities thus depends upon a prior training given with this end in view. Intentional agencies— schools—and explicit material— studies—are devised. The task of teaching certain things is delegated to a special group of persons.

—Dewey (1916)

sequentially moved through the "stations" (grades) on the assembly line. They spend a fixed amount of time at each one (a school year). If, at the end of the allotted time, they aren't "done," they are sorted into "streams" or "tracks" and moved to other parts of the building. This metaphor for schools has largely fit the times. Society has been content because it worked for most people. Many students left school for work at an early age, but this was not viewed as a problem. Those who left were not called "dropouts." There were legitimate places for the majority of young people to go that did not require much schooling—places like factories, mines, and places for farming and fishing. Assessment, in the form of classroom tests and final examinations, was the set of gates through which students had to pass to move to the next level of education. Education, beyond the basics, was a scarce resource, necessary only for a few.

Not everyone agreed that schools should be organizations to serve economic imperatives. Dewey, as early as 1916, wrote eloquently about the need for education to serve all students, and that education was necessary in order for society to continue to grow in democratic, social, and moral ways. However, the major model for schooling mimicked the industrial model of work, and teachers were the quality control agents who decided which of their students continued on to higher levels of schooling.

The rise of the middle class and capitalism in the middle of the century threw the social order into flux, and many groups began to demand equity in society. Schools were becoming the key to social mobility, and there was considerable pressure to ensure that decisions about access to advanced schooling were made based on merit, rather than social status. It was time for an efficient mechanism in schools to identify and categorize students so that they were placed in the appropriate slots—something that was based on predictions about their likely success in a range of future endeavors. Assessment of achievement became the basis for awarding of privileges, with tests and exams as the process used to sort the students in a way that satisfied the expectations held by the mainstream society and that would be accepted as fair. This kind of sorting became an important function of schools (Stiggins, 2001).

Although teachers were often involved in the testing process, there was considerable pressure for mechanisms that were not biased by the teachers' subjective judgment. There was also tremendous optimism about social science in general and mental testing in particular (Lemann, 1999). Don't forget, the Army Alpha had been enormously successful in selecting officer candidates for the military in World War I (Popham, 2002), and a whole range of mental measurements was being developed in its image.

In many countries, the focus moved to seemingly scientific and objective mechanisms for measuring student achievement. In some, examinations became the arbiter of admission to differential secondary education and to universities. In England, they established the 11+ examinations that consigned young people to their lifelong social fates at age 11. If they did well, they went to grammar schools. Otherwise, they stayed in the local comprehensive school. Entrance to university in England changed from a system of "friends at court" to success on A-level examinations. In Canada, provincial exit exams defined access to universities. The Baccalaureate in France did the same. In the United States, the SATs were developed for the same reasons. As Nicholas Lemann (1999) describes it, Henry Chauncey, the first president of the Educational Testing Service (ETS), had a plan:

> To depose the existing, undemocratic American elite and replace it with a new one made up of brainy, elaborately trained, public-spirited people drawn from every section and every background. (p. 5)

The mechanism for this transformation was the administration of a series of multiple-choice tests to everyone and, on the basis of the scores, deciding what each person's role in society should be. The SATs were born.

In all of these different contexts, external tests or examinations were the means by which the "gatekeepers" exercised power and gave the illusion, at least, of objective measurement. The important decisions about access to higher education were determined outside schools and classrooms using so-called scientifically developed instruments.

It is no surprise that the control embodied in the examinations filtered down to affect those who were anxious to provide their students with access. Assessment in schools quickly took on the summative role, designed not only to report the achievement of individuals to parents, other teachers, and the students themselves, but also to make decisions about student placements and life choices. Students were given different programs, sorted into different "tracks," and set on the voyage toward their various destinations. Assessment in schools became the local gatekeeper, emulating the external exam models and reinforcing the need to sort and select. Schools and teachers contributed to this process through a system of ongoing reporting, rewards and penalties, and program decisions.

Once again, however, other perspectives and voices were clamoring in the background. In 1971, Bloom, Hastings, and Madaus wrote a landmark book titled *Formative and Summative Evaluation of Student Learning* that described a view of education in which the primary purpose of schooling was the development of the individual. In their view, assessment and evaluation were a part of learning, and classroom teachers played a prominent role in using evaluation to improve and extend student learning. Although their work influenced a generation of teachers and administrators, their voices often have been overwhelmed by the power of testing as a mechanism for social control and social mobility.

Over time, in the United States in particular, external standardized testing took on a dominant role in this process of identifying and selecting students for favor or censure. Standardized tests offer an image of "scientific credibility" and have the advantage of being easily mass-produced, administered, and scored (Stiggins, 2001). Because of this concrete, apparently scientific mechanism for deriving scores that appear to have the same meaning for all students, standardized tests have dominated the landscape for more than 50 years. In the 1980s, a number of researchers and educators began to challenge the stranglehold of multiple-choice tests on education. There was evidence that multiple-choice tests could not assess a student's ability to produce answers, that mass-produced tests may not test what local schools are actually teaching, and that the tests push teachers into narrowing the curriculum until the test becomes the instruction (Barton, 1999). A great deal of debate occurred about the quality of tests and the implications of test use (Broadfoot, 1996; Haney, Madaus, & Lyons, 1993; Popham, 2002). Challenges and counterchallenges continue to keep many lawyers, bureaucrats, test makers, and educators employed and busy defending, devising, challenging, and changing standardized tests.

For many states and districts, the solution to the concerns was to demand or create more authentic assessments. They began using portfolio assessments or performance assessments meant to reflect more closely what is expected of students in the real world. New assessment systems were born. Some died early. Others have lived on. Some have been reversed, and others have been replaced.

Thousands of people have been involved in trying to get large-scale assessment right. Mountains of books and articles have been written about the various approaches to large-scale assessment and whether or not they work. The debates will undoubtedly continue. I do not intend to try to capture the content of the arguments about large-scale assessment, because that would be another book. I do want to note, however, that throughout the sometimes heated and rancorous debates, often focusing on the technical quality and merit of the tests, there has been remarkably little public discussion about the purpose of these assessments and how they contribute to student learning. In fact, although the rhetoric about educational reform always cites improvement as the goal, all too often, improvement is defined in terms of increased test scores, with little attention to what the scores represent in terms of learning. Because large-scale assessment has become the vehicle of choice for accountability purposes and the lever for holding schools accountable for results (Firestone, Mayrowetz, & Fairman, 1998), other purposes have fallen away. The stakes are too high. Superintendents, principals, teachers, and policymakers watch closely to see what has happened to the test scores. But who is watching student learning?

Looking for Change in All the Wrong Places

The persistent determination to use large-scale assessment as the primary lever for school reform may be fundamentally misdirected. Most of the rhetoric about school reform is about improving the quality of what schools do and, by inference, the quality of student learning. Standardized tests are intended to provide information for accountability, evaluation, or comparative purposes; focus public and media attention on educational concerns; and change educational practice and instruction (Haertel, 1999). Unfortunately, existing standardized tests and even large-scale performance assessments are remarkably insensitive to the detection of the things students have learned (McDonnell, 1994; Popham, 2002). They are designed to spread students out on a continuum, but they do not provide sufficient information to direct the work of schools or tell the people who work in them what to do next. Evidence is also emerging that large-scale assessment really doesn't change *how* teachers teach (Firestone, Winter, & Fitz, 2000), although some teachers and administrators have enhanced their scores by using the test as the curriculum or by tampering with test scores. The major influences of these massive assessment programs seem to be in making concerns about education visible to the public, supporting the political desire for accountability, and focusing attention on raising test scores. They are used to grade schools, scold schools, and judge whether schools are achieving their goals (Barton, 1999). Learning is not a central issue.

As many authors have described, educational change is much more complex than most reform agendas have allowed for, and many reforms have had very little impact on practice (Elmore, 1996; Fullan, 2000; Hargreaves et al., 2001). More than a decade ago, Larry Cuban (1988) at Stanford drew attention to a fundamental puzzle in school reform. He pointed out that through a whole century of rhetoric about school reform, the basics of schooling have remained remarkably similar. His explanation for this paradox is that reformers have concentrated largely on "first-order" changes—*changes that try to make what already exists more efficient and effective.* Very few reforms focused on "second-order" changes—*changes designed to alter the fundamental ways in which schools operate.* The few second-order changes that did emerge (e.g., open space, team teaching, flexible scheduling) were quickly diverted by teachers and administrators, who saw minimal gain and much loss in embracing the changes and either adapted them to fit what existed or ignored them (Cuban, 1988). Nevertheless, second-order changes are probably necessary if schools are going to prepare young people for a future in which they are required to be competent, confident, and creative learners as a starting point for dealing with the complexity of their lives.

Rethinking Assessment for Real Change

This book is about changing assessment in ways that will challenge the status quo. The ideas that are included clearly suggest second-order changes that will influence how teachers view their work and act on a daily basis in their classrooms, not just a few superficial changes in delivery or resources. This kind of change is hard. Cuban (1988) warned us that trying to implement second-order changes in schools can lead to a sense of impotence and pessimism. He also reminded us that fundamental changes can occur when teachers themselves believe that the changes are worth making and when there is a parallel change in the social and political structures that exist outside schools.

The history of assessment described above shows a long line of first-order changes designed to inject quality control into education using a testing system designed to measure student performance and hold schools accountable. We have been consumed with more frequent and rigorous testing as the obvious mechanism for improving schools. Even well-meaning reformers offer testing as a politically feasible solution to the problems in schools. Unfortunately, criticizing educators does not improve schools, and higher test scores do not equal higher standards or better learning. Although policymakers often find ways to straddle the fence, educators are independent actors who can wield their own influence in their classrooms and schools. The time may be right for rethinking assessment in schools.

In a recent editorial in the journal *Assessment in Education,* Patricia Broadfoot (2001) bemoaned the fact that

> Current developments in society are set within a context that is characterised by a confused muddle of institutions and practices that are the enduring product of previous eras. Such institutions and practices were, more often than not, conceived in response to very different social and economic priorities of the past. Not surprisingly, their continuing contemporary influence can provide a significant drag on our collective capacity to address present day challenges. We cling to the familiar like a much-loved old garment, even when it is long past its best and ought to have been discarded long ago. (p. 109)

Assessment, as she points out later, is one of these muddled processes in transition from the past. Government policies are routinely placing conflicting demands on schools. This is not an indictment of government. Rather, it is a genuine reflection of a society divided about what schools are for. Much of the debate (both overt and hidden) in education focuses on the purpose of schooling. Some legislation is premised on schools as instruments of social control that need to be controlled themselves. Large-scale assessment, sanctions, and incentives for schools are a visible example. Other legislative directions identify schools as the mechanism for maximizing opportunities for all, with rhetoric about fairness and equity. At the same time that there is an increasing focus on accountability, there is also a societal push toward enhancing learning for all students.

Schools and districts are caught in an era with the contradictory purposes of "education for all" and "education as gatekeeper" with control of the nature of goals and rewards. Teachers and administrators are the instruments of these contradictory demands and are both recipients and perpetrators of these competing messages.

Despite the amount of research evidence that testifies to the shortcomings of many assessment techniques as a means of measuring educational achievement, existing assessment practices are so deeply rooted in our collective intellectual and political consciousness that they have been almost impossible to challenge. They may even become more entrenched as policymakers realize the power of large-scale assessment to monitor, compare, and leverage educational systems.

In this confused and emotionally charged assessment environment, the stakes are high to "get it right." Educators find themselves in a difficult position. They are part of the transition, laden down with the burdens of the past, while contemplating the possibilities of the future. They know how it has always been and have a great deal invested in maintaining stability, but at the same time, many of them acknowledge that it just doesn't feel right. What better way to bring some clarity to a murky subject than to return to first principles: What is our purpose? What are we trying to accomplish? What is assessment for?

Purpose Is Everything

As I and others have written about elsewhere, classroom assessment has a multitude of purposes, many of them contradictory. In a book about reinventing education for young adolescents (Hargreaves, Earl, & Ryan, 1996), we discussed the multiple and competing purposes of assessment as the motivation of students, the diagnosis of difficulties, certification of achievement, and accountability to the public. In our discussion, we draw attention to the paradoxes and contradictions inherent in trying to fulfill all of these purposes together. For example, traditional classroom assessment and reporting processes permit comparisons among students, fulfill accountability demands, and certify students for entry into other educational programs or institutions. But they do not provide any specific information about what the student has achieved. Diagnostic assessment cannot occur when a test event is high-stakes. Why would a student take the risk of making errors or showing misunderstanding to a teacher if the result is likely to work to the student's disadvantage?

Paul Black (1998) identified three broad purposes of assessment in schools: support learning; report achievement of individuals for certification, progress, and transfer; and satisfy the demands for public accountability. He goes on to point out that tensions among these purposes involve choices about (a) the best agencies to conduct assessments and (b) the optimum instruments and appropriate interpretations to serve each purpose.

Rick Stiggins (2001), in a discussion of standardized testing, points out that we have been relentless in our attempts to make standardized tests powerful instructional tools that are relevant in the classroom. Unfortunately, such tests tend to provide little information of value for day-to-day instruction. They do a good job of assessing broad classifications of content and spreading students out on the basis of the scores (considered against a reference point of other students or specific, preset standards) so that they can be sorted into groups. They do not provide timely or sufficient information to inform classroom practice.

In all of these discussions, the theme is the same. It is not possible to use one assessment process for the many purposes that we want it to fulfill. Different purposes require vastly different approaches, and mixing the purposes is likely to ensure that none of them will be well served. It is becoming more and more obvious that we must first decide about the purpose and then design the assessment program to fit (Gipps, 1994).

Like learning and teaching, assessment is not a singular entity. It is complex and dynamic, and it deserves to be differentiated and understood in all of its intricacy. Educators need to think about the various purposes for assessment and make choices about the purposes

> Using one assessment for a multitude of purposes is like using a hammer for everything from brain-surgery to pile driving.
>
> —Walt Haney (1991)

that they believe are important and how to realize these purposes every day in their classrooms. The good news in this story is that many other educators and researchers have been thinking, writing, and talking about these ideas for some time. Strong voices have been emerging with alternative visions for assessment in schools—visions that make purpose paramount and shift the focus from large-scale assessments for accountability to classroom assessment for teaching and learning. Many others agree with Linda Darling-Hammond (1994), who envisions an era in which the goal of schooling is to educate all children well, rather than selecting a "talented tenth" to be prepared for knowledge work. This new era will be one in which it is no longer sufficient for schools to sort their students and cull out the ones who don't fit the school's recipe for learning. Instead, learning will be the fundamental purpose of schooling (Earl & Cousins, 1995).

Since the mid-1980s, there has been a steady stream of advocates for assessment being educationally useful (Black, 1998; Gipps, 1994; Popham, 1995; Shepard, 1989; Stiggins, 1991; Sutton, 1995; Wiggins, 1993; Wiggins & McTighe, 1999; Wolf, Bixby, Glenn, & Gardner, 1991). They, and others, have focused on the importance and value of the assessment that teachers do every day in classrooms as a critical element in helping students learn. A great deal has been written already about these alternative images of classroom assessment, and teachers flock to professional development sessions to learn about new ways to perform assessment. Still, the practices that are being advocated are more the exception than the rule and are not encouraged or supported in many educational settings.

But the seeds have been sown for a genuine revolution, and ideas are there to be nurtured and to blossom. This assessment revolution is not happening in the halls of power, although governments can assist in its development and hasten its influence, if they so choose. Instead, assessment is situated in schools and particularly in classrooms, as students and teachers work together. The shift that these various authors envision depends on teachers and others rethinking how and why assessment and teaching happen.

Lorrie Shepard (2000) worried aloud, in her presidential address to the American Educational Research Association, that external accountability testing can lead to deskilling and deprofessionalizing of teachers and will teach students and teachers that effort in school should be in response to externally mandated rewards and punishments, rather than the excitement of ideas. I agree. However, I also worry that moves to empower teachers to take back assessment will result in reinforcement of the traditions that Broadfoot (2001) mentioned—traditions of teachers judging students using questionable methods, without the changes in assessment purpose or approach that will make it an integral part of learning. Just moving assessment back to teachers' control, on its own, is not a positive change. Returning to some fictional golden age will not move the agenda forward. Even when they were relatively autonomous, teachers retained control mainly of their own "secret gardens." More recently, they have been victims of change. Teachers should and can be agents of change, not victims. But the road is long and likely difficult.

The revolution is much larger than just assessment. It is a revolution about learning. And the purpose is very clear—high-level learning for all students. Approaching this vision of schools as learning institutions requires a dramatic change in the assumptions underlying education, and it requires a different view of schools, schooling, teachers, teaching, and, particularly, assessment. In this conception, *schools* have the responsibility for preparing *all* students for tomorrow's world; *teachers* have the wherewithal to guide all students to high levels of learning; and, *assessment,* first and foremost, is part of student learning. This seemingly straightforward shift requires dramatic changes in the way teaching and learning happen in schools.

After researching almost 7,000 classrooms across the United States, from 1900 to 1980, Cuban (1984) reported that most of the teachers taught the entire class as a group, with classroom activities built around students listening, writing, and watching. He suggested that this approach was consistent with societal expectations:

> The overriding purposes of the school . . . are to inculcate in children the prevailing social norms, values and behaviors that will prepare them for participation in the larger culture. . . . Those teaching practices that seek obedience, uniformity, productivity, and other traits required for minimum participation in bureaucratic and industrial organizations, are viewed as both necessary and worthwhile. . . . As the students grow older, homework, tests and grades focus on classroom

competitiveness and productivity.... Certain teaching practices are functional: whole-group instruction where waving hands vie for teachers attention; a question-answer format that rewards those better at factual recall; classroom furniture arranged to produce a uniform appearance; textbooks, a primary source of knowledge, yield reams of homework to which credit is given or withheld and becomes the basis for tests and quizzes. Dominant teaching practices, then, endure because they produce student behaviors consistent with the requirements of the larger society especially in the high school. (pp. 240–241)

So, changing classroom assessment is the beginning of a revolution— a revolution in classroom practices of all kinds. A tall order, but not an impossible one. Educational change is a process of creeping incrementalism, with tiny changes, day after day, in many different and unpredictable ways and places. We have already taken many of these first steps and made many of the tiny changes. We are embarking on an evolutionary path toward the revolution. Over time, teachers, parents, and students can re-form the nature of assessment in schools from a culture of judging and categorizing to one that fosters learning for all.

Taking Up the Challenge

In the current climate, educators are uniquely positioned to make fundamental changes in the purposes and processes of assessment in their classrooms, but it will not be an easy road. Powerful forces are operating in several different directions. The push of large-scale reform is for more centralized control, with national or state curricula and concomitant testing systems. At the same time, the veneer over teachers' moral purpose is very thin. Most of them entered the profession to make a difference in students' lives, and they are routinely concerned about how to serve their students well. When students are at stake, many teachers are willing to consider new approaches. The public is still undecided and probably uninformed as well. They need images of another way, of alternatives to what has always been.

Although the challenges are immense, this is not a time for inertia. As one of my favorite cartoon characters, Pogo, once said: "We seem to be surrounded by insurmountable opportunities." Teachers and administrators have the potential to use assessment as an exciting and powerful means for enhancing learning. Getting classroom assessment right is not a simplistic, either-or situation. It is a complex mix of challenging personal beliefs, rethinking instruction, and learning new ways to assess for different purposes. It requires educators who are excited about learning, imaginative, and willing to formulate strategies of "resistance" that allow them to use assessment in productive ways in their classrooms and honor the complexity of learning and assessment. None of the assessment purposes described above is right or wrong. They are situational. They work in different ways under different conditions.

Oddly enough, the large-scale reform agendas of the past decade provide the possibility of movement toward a different kind of classroom assessment, assessment that is more consistent with alternative images than is obvious at first glance.

Classroom Assessment and Large-Scale Reform

Education is in the foreground of many legislative agendas, and many governments have embarked on large-scale reform agendas designed to change entire systems. As Michael Fullan (2000) describes it, "Large-scale reform has returned with a vengeance" (p. 19). Over the past decade, large-scale reform has been surprisingly similar around the world. Geoff Whitty and his colleagues (Whitty, Power, & Halpin, 1998) studied legislative changes to education in Australia, England, Wales, New Zealand, Sweden, and the United States. Each country had its unique history and context, but the various governments had introduced policies that sought to reformulate the relationship between government, schools, and parents. All involved increased responsibility for individual schools, a reduction of power for district school boards or local education authorities, more power and responsibility to parents, changes to and centralization of curriculum, the introduction of standards or expectations for student learning, and centralized assessment schemes.

When governments mandate reform agendas, they are generally focused on first-order changes that are intended to put pressure on schools through external quality control, with scores from large-scale assessment as the ultimate measure of success. All too often, educators deplore and resist the changes or engage in superficial compliance to satisfy their masters. In my mind, this process is a diversion that takes us away from the work at hand. However, the current wave of large-scale reform contains much of value that can be cultivated and colonized by educators to transform the first-order changes into second-order changes, particularly in relation to learning, teaching, and assessment; second-order changes designed to change the very fabric of what schools are for.

Table 2.1   Characteristics of Large-Scale Reform

- Vision and goals
- Standards
- Curriculum frameworks and other teaching resources
- Focus on teaching and learning
- Accountability and incentives based on performance
- Coherent and integrated policies
- Sufficient funding and workable governance structures

SOURCE: Leithwood et al. (1999).

In a recent review of characteristics of large-scale reform, Leithwood, Jantzi, and Mascall (1999) identified the elements that seem to be present in most large-scale reform efforts. Their headings are displayed in Table 2.1.

The authors go on to say that, even with all these dimensions, change is not likely to happen in schools unless teachers are motivated to change, have the capacity to make the changes, and work in a context where support is readily available. In this section, I've taken the characteristics that they have identified and offered suggestions for how they can become the basis for exciting and serious change in schools, founded on the simple assumptions that permeate this text.

Vision and Goals

Most reform initiatives purport to be about enhancing student learning. The rhetoric about high standards for all and no child left behind provides a perfect starting point for educators to make learning the fundamental purpose of schools and to focus all of their efforts in that direction. What could be more worthy of attention in schools than quality learning for every student?

Standards

Virtually every state, province, and country has or is engaged in setting standards or expectations for student learning. Standards may be the reference point for large-scale assessments, but they are also the best descriptions available of what we expect of students in schools. Standards can make the work of schools visible to the public that they serve and give students clear learning targets. The process of looking at actual student work, discussing expected levels of achievement, and setting standards can lead to a constructive dialogue about what should be taught in schools and at what level. In particular, the active involvement of teachers and the public in writing standards has developed alliances among educators and the public in the struggle to define directions for education for children. Even more compelling is the fact that learning is easier when both the teacher and the student have a clear image of where they are headed (Black and Wiliam, 1998). Standards offer the basis for describing the expectations and making them concrete and accessible to everyone.

Curriculum Frameworks and Resources

Curriculum frameworks, when they do not become straitjackets for teachers, provide the backdrop for consistency and rigor in what gets taught. One of the most salient complaints about education has been the lack of consistency in what gets taught and how well it is taught from one district to another, one school to another, and one classroom to another. The current wave of reform has brought the essentials of curriculum into center stage. Virtually all of the reform-driven curriculum frameworks have a major focus on early literacy and numeracy. This renewed focus is quite different from the 3Rs of our past. In the 21st century, it is essential that all children (and eventually all adults) have solid facility with language and numbers, as well as many other more sophisticated skills. Children need concepts of literacy and numeracy so that they can move from *learning how* to read, write, and work with numbers to *using* reading, writing, and mathematics as tools to learn in other areas and to communicate their ideas to others.

This is not to suggest that literacy and numeracy are the only building blocks for learning. They are essential for future learning, but they are not all that young children need to learn, nor should they displace other important learning. They can use the symbol systems of language and numbers to develop competence and expertise in other areas by engaging in the learning work of developing and internalizing knowledge, organizing knowledge in a broad range of areas of study, and connecting ideas together in ways that make sense. This requires facility with the conventions, knowledge, concepts, and ideas embedded in the particular discipline, as well as comfort with a whole range of ways of thinking about and analyzing them.

When governments and teachers' associations produce curriculum documents, they provide teachers not with a roadmap to follow slavishly, but with a framework to inform their practice and challenge their conceptions of what ought to be included. When the work of producing curriculum is a collaborative effort that includes expert teachers, teachers are able to spend their valuable time refining and adjusting the material for use in their setting.

Focus on Teaching and Learning

Success in large-scale reform is related to the extent to which the reforms focus on teaching and learning. Teachers may resent the implications that they do not focus on teaching and learning already. Unfortunately, many things happen in schools that divert attention from learning. Even when it is a central purpose, there is always more that can be done. When teachers and students make learning the ultimate goal, their actions are not only consistent with the reforms but also deeply connected to the moral purpose of schooling. There may appear to be many hurdles, but nothing needs to stand in the way of making learning paramount.

Accountability and Incentives
Based on Performance

Although accountability in policy terms is often defined by standardized test scores and target setting, accountability for teachers and students can be shown directly, every day, in the work that they do and the learning that occurs. Incentives in this case are not just extrinsic rewards. They emerge from the recognition of successful action and the knowledge that it came from personal commitment and hard work. The rewards are in the satisfaction of learning that is well done.

Coherent and Integrated Policies

When governments manage to align their policies in relation to things like curriculum and special education so that there is clear direction for schools, educators have less to unravel in order to integrate the policies into schools and classrooms and can concentrate on learning and teaching.

Sufficient Funding and Workable
Governance Structures

These final components of large-scale reform efforts are certainly important dimensions for making implementation of reforms easier. They can also be assets for engaging in assessment reform in schools. At the same time, they may not be essential if teachers and administrators have the will and the determination to embark on the kinds of second-order changes that are described in this book.

Often, the opportunities embedded in large-scale reform are difficult to see, even when the reforms are well intentioned. Considering reforms dispassionately can be particularly hard when teachers feel denigrated, devalued, and under scrutiny. It seems that every intended outcome of a policy comes with its shadow of unintended outcomes, and the eclipse caused by the shadow is sometimes more dramatic than the original image. This being the case, teachers and administrators have it in their power to act rather than react and to move the educational change agenda forward in ways that they believe can really benefit students.

Ideas for Follow-Up

1.   What was the purpose of classroom assessment when you were a student?

2.   How is *large-scale assessment* being used for educational change in your district?

3.   How is *classroom assessment* being used for educational change in your district?

Assessment *of* Learning, *for* Learning, and *as* Learning

In Chapter 1, I described a "preferred future" for assessment. My vision is one that makes assessment an integral part of learning—guiding the process and stimulating further learning. The word *assessment* is derived from the Latin *assidere*, meaning "to sit beside or with" (Wiggins, 1993). Although this notion of a teacher sitting with her students to really understand what is happening as they pursue the challenges of learning is far removed from the role that assessment and evaluation have typically played in schools, many teachers have always done it. In this chapter, I look more closely at the various purposes for assessment that occurs routinely in classrooms. Classroom assessment is a complex undertaking that means something different to different audiences and in different situations. And so it should. Assessment has many purposes that sometimes support one another and sometimes compete or conflict with one another. As Wilson (1996) noted, teachers engage in a broad range of assessment roles, and keeping them straight is a challenging task (see Table 3.1).

Clearly, these roles overlap, and watching teachers try to manage the assessment activities and juggle them to satisfy the various goals shows how complex the process of classroom assessment really is. Also, tensions are embedded in these various roles and goals that cause concern for teachers. I hope that these tensions become more visible and understandable after I describe three different approaches to classroom assessment that have guided my thinking as I have contemplated the role of classroom assessment in my preferred future. The three approaches are Assessment *of* Learning, Assessment *for* Learning, and Assessment *as* Learning. Although I intend to highlight the contribution of Assessment *for* Learning and Assessment *as* Learning as part of a preferred future, Assessment *of* Learning is also

Table 3.1   Assessment Roles and Goals

Role	Goal
Teacher as mentor	Provide feedback and support to each student.
Teacher as guide	Gather diagnostic information to lead the group through the work at hand.
Teacher as accountant	Maintain records of student progress and achievement.
Teacher as reporter	Report to parents, students, and the school administration about student progress and achievement.
Teacher as program director	Make adjustments and revisions to instructional practices.

SOURCE: Adapted from *Assessment Roles and Goals* (Wilson, 1996).

valuable and has its place. In my mind, it is important to understand them all, recognize the inevitable contradictions among them, know which one you are using and why, and use them all wisely and well.

Assessment *of* Learning

The predominant kind of assessment in schools is Assessment *of* Learning. Its purpose is summative, intended to certify learning and report to parents and students about students' progress in school, usually by signaling students' relative position compared to other students. Assessment *of* Learning in classrooms is typically done at the end of something (e.g., a unit, a course, a grade, a Key Stage, a program) and takes the form of tests or exams that include questions drawn from the material studied during that time. In Assessment *of* Learning, the results are expressed symbolically, generally as marks or letter grades, and summarized as averages of a number of marks across several content areas to report to parents.

This is the kind of assessment that still dominates most classroom assessment activities, especially in secondary schools, with teachers firmly in charge of both creating and marking the tests. Teachers use the tests to assess the quantity and accuracy of student work, and the bulk of teacher effort in assessment is taken up in marking and grading. A strong emphasis is placed on comparing students, and feedback to students comes in the form of marks or grades, with little direction or advice for improvement. These kinds of testing events indicate which students are doing well and which ones are doing poorly. Typically, they don't give much indication of mastery of particular ideas or concepts because the test content is generally too limited and the scoring is too simplistic to represent the broad range of skills and knowledge that has been covered. But this lack of specificity hasn't presented a problem because the teachers' perceived purpose of the assessment is to produce a rank order of the students and assign a symbol to designate the students' position within the group, whatever group it might be. Teachers maintain voluminous records of student achievement that are used only for justifying the grades that are assigned.

Although much of this book focuses on the next two approaches to assessment, there are and will always be milestones and junctures where "summative" assessment is called for and Assessment *of* Learning is essential. Doing it right is a challenge in itself.

Assessment *of* Learning and grading have a long history in education. They have been widely accepted by parents and the public. If they have served us so well, why would we worry about a process that works? Without moving too far away from my primary purpose, I'd like to highlight a few of the issues that are currently contentious about what we have always done. Although the public has been largely supportive of grading in schools, skepticism is increasing about its fairness and even its accuracy. Educational researchers and theorists have been critical of traditional grading practices for quite some time (Marzano, 2000). In terms of measurement theory, grades are highly suspect. Why? Because teachers consider many factors other than academic achievement when they assign grades; teachers weight assessments differently, and they misinterpret single scores on assessments to represent performance on a wide range of skills and abilities (Marzano, 2000). As education becomes an essential ingredient for a successful future, more attention will be paid to how grades are calculated and how well they actually reflect what they are taken to mean.

The book is not yet closed on Assessment *of* Learning, and educators have a great deal to learn to ensure that it and the grades that result from it are defensible and worthwhile.

> To measure or to learn; that is the question.
>
> —Broadfoot (1996)

Assessment *for* Learning

Assessment *for* Learning offers an alternative perspective to traditional assessment in schools. Simply put, Assessment *for* Learning shifts the emphasis from summative to formative assessment, from making judgments to creating descriptions that can be used in the service of the next stage of learning.

When they are doing Assessment *for* Learning, teachers collect a wide range of data so that they can modify the learning work for their students. They craft assessment tasks that open a window on what students know and can do already and use the insights that come from the process to design the next steps in instruction. To do this, teachers use observation, worksheets, questioning in class, student-teacher conferences, or whatever mechanism is likely to give them information that will be useful for their planning and teaching. Marking is not designed to make comparative judgments among the students but to highlight each student's strengths and weaknesses and provide them with feedback that will further their learning.

> Assumption: Classroom assessment can enhance learning.

Clearly, teachers are the central characters in Assessment *for* Learning as well, but their role is quite different from that in the prior approach. In Assessment *for* Learning, they use their personal knowledge of the students and their understanding of the context of the assessment and the curriculum targets to identify particular learning needs. Assessment *for* Learning happens in the middle of learning, often more than once, rather than at the end. It is interactive, with teachers providing assistance as part of the assessment. It helps teachers provide the feedback to scaffold next steps. And it depends on teachers' diagnostic skills to make it work.

> When the cook tastes the soup, that's formative; when the guests taste the soup, that's summative.
>
> —Robert Stake

Recordkeeping in this approach may include a grade book, but the records on which teachers rely are things like checklists of student progress against expectations, artifacts, portfolios of student work over time, and worksheets to trace the progression of students along the learning continuum.

> In reality, it is through classroom assessment that attitudes, skills, knowledge and thinking are fostered, nurtured and accelerated – or stifled.
>
> —Hynes (1991)

Assessment *as* Learning

Assessment *for* Learning can go a long way in enhancing student learning. By introducing the notion of Assessment *as* Learning,

I intend to reinforce and extend the role of formative assessment for learning by emphasizing the role of the student, not only as a contributor to the assessment and learning process, but also as the critical connector between them. The student is the link. Students, as active, engaged, and critical assessors, can make sense of information, relate it to prior knowledge, and master the skills involved. This is the regulatory process in metacognition. It occurs when students personally monitor what they are learning and use the feedback from this monitoring to make adjustments, adaptations, and even major changes in what they understand. Assessment *as* Learning is the ultimate goal, where students are their own best assessors.

At some point, students will need to be self-motivating and able to bring their talents and knowledge to bear on the decisions and problems that make up their lives. They can't just wait for the | Assumption: Self-assessment is at the heart of the matter.

teacher (or politicians, or salespeople, or religious leaders) to tell them whether or not the answer is "right." Effective assessment empowers students to ask reflective questions and consider a range of strategies for learning and acting. Over time, students move forward in their learning when they can use personal knowledge to construct meaning, have skills of self-monitoring to realize that they don't understand something, and have ways of deciding what to do next.

Recordkeeping in Assessment *as* Learning is a personal affair. Students and teachers decide (often together) about the important evidence of learning and how it should be organized and kept. Students routinely reflect on their work and make judgments about how they can capitalize on what they have done already. Comparison with others is almost irrelevant. Instead, the critical reference points are the student's own prior work and the aspirations and targets for continued learning.

Getting the Balance Right

These three approaches all contribute to student learning but in vastly different ways. Table 3.2 gives a summary of the salient features of each approach.

As I mentioned earlier, all three assessment approaches have their place. The trick is to get the balance right. At the current juncture, almost all classroom assessment in a traditional environment is summative Assessment *of* Learning, focused on measuring learning after the fact and used for categorizing students and reporting these judgments to others. A few teachers use Assessment *for* Learning by building in diagnostic processes—formative assessment and feedback

Table 3.2   Features of Assessment *of, for*, and *as* Learning

Approach	Purpose	Reference Points	Key Assessor
Assessment *of* Learning	Judgments about placement, promotion, credentials, etc.	Other students	Teacher
Assessment *for* Learning	Information for teachers' instructional decisions	External standards or expectations	Teacher
Assessment *as* Learning	Self-monitoring and self-correction or adjustment	Personal goals and external standards	Student

at stages in the program—and giving students second chances to improve their marks (and, it is hoped, their learning). Systematic Assessment *as* Learning is almost nonexistent.

Obviously, there are times when information about students' achievement of key outcomes and the degree to which they compare with others is important and the approach should be Assessment *of* Learning. The issue is whether schools should be utilizing Assessment *of* Learning over and over again to such an extent that it leaves no place for other approaches to assessment. Figure 3.1 shows this traditional relationship of the approaches to one another.

Figure 3.2 shows a reconfiguration of the pyramid to suggest a different kind of balance—one that emphasizes increased attention to Assessment *for* and *as* Learning. In this scenario, Assessment *of* Learning has a role to play when decisions must be made that require summative judgments, or when teachers and students want to see the cumulative effect of their work, but this role is relatively small. The major focus is on classroom assessment that contributes to student learning, by the teacher (for learning) and by the student (as learning).

Given the history of schools as sorting institutions, the notion that assessment and learning are intimately and inextricably intertwined is revolutionary. On the surface of it, the ideas are appealing, but the fit with schools as we know them is uncomfortable and awkward. I suspect this is the dilemma that teachers have talked about when they say, "Assessment is the hardest part." They have always been caught between monitoring learning and categorizing students on the basis of their assessments, and teaching students, and they have struggled with these contradictory responsibilities. One teacher whom I interviewed recently expressed it this way:

Figure 3.1   Traditional Assessment Pyramid

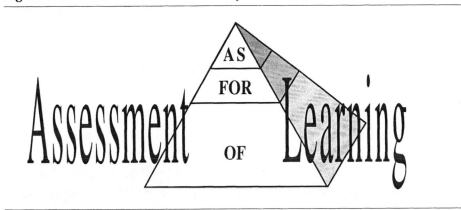

Figure 3.2   Reconfigured Assessment Pyramid

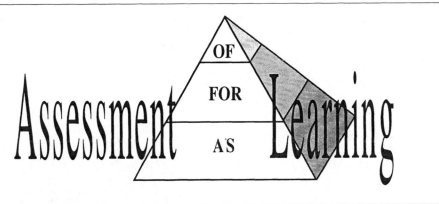

> I really struggle with assessment. I'm supposed to be teaching for mastery of learning skills. What does that have to do with common testing?

This tension, which has always existed, is exactly the reason for reconfiguring the balance. Teachers and administrators can implement this reconfiguration without creating a major upheaval in what the community, especially parents, expect of schools. Parents always have their own children's interests at heart. When they can see how Assessment *for* and *as* Learning can contribute to enhanced learning and success for their child, it may draw them into the fray as willing allies in the focus on learning.

In this reconfigured assessment environment, assessment would make up a large part of the school day, not in the form of separate tests, but as a seamless part of the learning process. And there would be tests when the decisions to be made require identification of a few individuals or groups, or when a summative description is important for students and others as a milestone or rite of passage. In the real world, these incidents are far fewer than the experience of schools would lead us to believe.

Ideas for Follow-Up

1.   Interview teachers in your school to identify the balance of purposes for assessment. What does the assessment pyramid look like?

2.   Analyze samples of assessment tasks being used in your school. Are they designed to be Assessment *of, for,* or *as* Learning?

CHAPTER 4

A Focus on Learning

The underlying idea behind this book is that learning is the imperative. Learning has always provided the advantage for human survival through difficult, even seemingly impossible times. Human beings are able to learn, unlearn, share their learning, and pass on learning to those who follow. Learning is at the core of our being, as individuals and collectively. It is the key to equipping future generations to respond and to survive in a frenetically and unpredictably changing world. And perhaps most important, *we have not even approached the limits of what can be learned.*

The challenge for educators is to apply our emerging understanding about learning to help students become the citizens for a "preferred future" where all students, not just a

Assumption: Learning is the imperative in schools.

few, will learn. They will learn not only the foundation skills of language and mathematics, but also a whole range of "new basics," such as accessing, interpreting, and applying information; performing critical thinking and analysis; solving novel problems; making informed judgments; working independently and in groups; and discerning the appropriate course of action in ambiguous situations.

Learning is intellectual. Learning is social. Learning is emotional. It is ordered, and it is erratic. It happens by design and by chance. We all do it, and we take it for granted, even though we do not have a clear understanding of what it means or how to make the most of it.

There are a multiplicity of conceptions of the nature of learning, from something that *happens to* the learner, with knowledge as the "stuff" to fill students' waiting minds, to a view suggesting that learning is a completely unique experience of constructing reality for each

Figure 4.1   What Makes Humans Human?

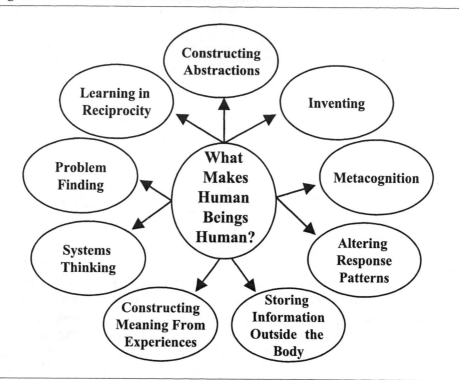

SOURCE: Stoll, Fink, and Earl (2002) (adapted from Costa, 1996).

individual. Clearly, learning is a complex and mysterious process that continues to challenge our understanding. In the past 50 years, however, we have learned a great deal that can and is being applied in classrooms. Figure 4.1, adapted from work by Costa (1996), shows the powerful and unique learning qualities that human beings have at their disposal for harnessing information and making sense of the world.

These human qualities that Costa (1996) outlined are the foundation of our ability to learn.

• *Metacognition.* Human beings can reflect on their own thinking processes. Experts describe such thinking as an internal conversation—monitoring their own understanding, predicting their performance, deciding what else they need to know, organizing and reorganizing ideas, checking for consistency between different pieces of information, and drawing analogies that help them advance their understanding.

• *Constructing abstraction.* Humans have the capacity to use language, images, and numbers as symbols to transform events into categories and patterns. These symbolic systems make it possible for people to think in abstractions and to order and reorder the world in thought.

• *Storing information outside the body.* Humans store, organize, and retrieve information in and from locations other than their bodies. From cave drawings, to books, to videodisks, external storage and retrieval systems provide access to information far beyond the limits of memory.

• *Systems thinking.* Humans are able to see patterns, congruencies, and inconsistencies while still focusing on the whole. This capacity allows them to consider many perspectives and to imagine how changing one element can have an impact on the total system.

• *Problem finding.* Not only are humans able to search for problems to solve, but they also appear to enjoy it. Humans question and sense ambiguities and anomalies in the world around them. Once there is some doubt, they look for better ways of understanding the nature of things.

• *Reciprocal learning.* Human beings are social creatures with a compulsive craving to engage with each other. They learn best in groups as they listen to one another, strive for agreement, and rethink their beliefs and understanding.

• *Inventing.* Human beings are creative and often motivated intrinsically, rather than extrinsically, to work on tasks because of the challenge. They constantly strive for greater fluency, elaboration, novelty, parsimony, simplicity, craftsmanship, perfection, harmony, beauty, and balance.

• *Deriving meaning from experience.* One of the most significant attributes of human beings is that they can reflect on and learn from their experiences. They can stand back, monitor activities, and modify actions or beliefs.

• *Altering response patterns.* Although a certain amount of human activity may be hard-wired, people are able to make significant conscious and deliberate choices about their behavior. They are always capable of learning and altering their responses based on new ideas or understanding.

Costa's (1996) framework accentuates the view that learning is not a static trait. It is a dynamic process that can be learned and developed as we go through the iterative process of fitting information into patterns or schema of similarities, differences, likeness, and regularities. The human mind operates by constructing something like a mental map, an internal representation allowing the individual to retrieve information efficiently and use it by making connections to other ideas. As learning progresses, learners move beyond the basic rules associated with any field until it becomes automatic, when they are comfortable in a domain, and when they begin to build their own understanding by acting, assessing what happens, reflecting, designing new strategies, and acting again. This is the "stuff" of classrooms and schools.

Although large-scale reform efforts often give the illusion that learning can be directed from outside, it is important to remember that things like centralized curriculum, testing programs, targetsetting, and inspections are all means to an end. And the end, I believe, is learning—better learning and more learning for all students.

In a recent book, *It's About Learning (And It's About Time)* (Stoll et al., 2002), several colleagues and I have described the changing nature of our knowledge about learning and how this knowledge can be channeled into new learning at all levels in education—students, teachers, leaders, schools, and educational systems. As you read this section, imagine some possible implications for assessment.

Learning for Understanding

Learning is not a passive process. Young minds are not empty of ideas and ready to receive our wisdom any more than adult minds are sponges absorbing new ideas from the air. From the earliest days, the minds of infants are active and toiling to make sense of the world around them. Over time, this sense-making activity is made up of conscious attention, organizing and reorganizing ideas, assimilating or accommodating new ideas, and constantly reshuffling and reorganizing in efforts to connect ideas into coherent patterns. Learning begins with some level of *consciousness* when someone focuses attention on it or because something about it commands attention. Once something enters consciousness, the human mind goes to work to organize it and connect it to what the mind already knows. This involves processing the information, searching for and retrieving information from memory or experience, checking the match between the new information and prior knowledge, monitoring comprehension, reorganizing ideas, and coming to decisions about what the new information means and where it fits. All of this activity happens at lightning speed; generally, the learner is completely unaware of the process. Somehow, the wealth of information existing outside a person becomes part of an individual's internal "knowing."

When the new information is largely consistent with prior ideas and beliefs, it usually combines easily with existing knowledge and reinforces the existing views. If the new information is inconsistent or in conflict with existing ideas, the learner may be required to transform his or her beliefs. When this happens, the learner experiences dissonance and disorder, and needs sustained attention and energy to keep going. This is not just a cognitive process; it is emotional, because every piece of information gets evaluated for its bearing on the self and the potential effect on the learner's environment. Even though the dissonance causes discomfort, it is essential for conceptual change and, therefore, serious learning. Learning results from these episodes of dissonance (Linn & Songer, 1991; Olsen & Bruner, 1996).

In his book *Smart Schools: From Training Memories to Educating Minds*, David Perkins (1992) makes the bold statement that we already know enough about how learning works, how teachers teach, and how to cope with diversity to do a much

> New insights don't happen by osmosis. They come from facing ideas that challenge the familiar ways of viewing issues.
>
> —Earl and Katz (2002)

better job of educating. His claim comes in response to one of the most dramatic discoveries in learning research—that being able to recall and even apply concepts doesn't necessarily mean that the ideas have been understood. Most students, including the best students in the best schools, don't really understand (Gardner, 1991). All too often, children learn how to plug numbers into a formula or memorize descriptions of complex phenomena, but when they encounter the concepts in a new situation, they do not know how to use them. Material is kept in memory and drawn out (often erroneously) when it might fit. Unfortunately, students often know far more than they understand about subjects they have studied and suffer from many misconceptions or misunderstandings (Perkins & Unger, 2000).

Learning for understanding suggests a much deeper grasp of underlying ideas and concepts, not just recitation of algorithms or rules. Understanding is knowledge in action. Students who understand can take knowledge, concepts, skills, and facts and apply them in new situations where they are appropriate. Brandsford and colleagues (Brandsford, Brown, & Cocking, 1999) provide an example using Einstein's theory of relativity that should resonate for many of you. What would constitute evidence that someone understood $E = MC^2$? Reciting the equation only shows that it has been remembered; it does not show that it has been understood. Understanding involves knowledge about energy, mass, velocity of light, and mathematical notions such as "squaring." But this isn't enough. One would have to be able to use these concepts according to rules of physics, support the theory with evidence, identify the problems the theory solves and the theories it replaces, and so on. Deep understanding is having a grasp of the structure of a discipline, seeing how things are related, using the ideas in novel situations, and evaluating, even challenging, the knowledge claims embedded in the discipline.

Prior knowledge of a topic or idea provides the foundation for linking new ideas and building complex mental models, but as the Einstein example shows, knowledge in itself doesn't guarantee understanding. People need a rich base of knowledge about the subjects under consideration and a great deal of experience to become comfortable with the ideas and create the mental models that organize them.

Studies that examine differences between experts and novices have provided enormous insights into how knowledge and understanding work together (Brandsford et al., 1999). Certainly, novices possess less knowledge than experts, and less skill. But it is not merely the amount of knowledge or the number of skills that distinguishes experts from their less experienced peers. Experts also have well-honed regulatory systems that come into play when they become aware that something (facts or skills) is missing or doesn't fit. They display planning, control, and reflection in their actions. They are aware of the knowledge and skills that they possess, or are lacking, and use a range of strategies to actively implement them or acquire them (Ertmer & Newby, 1996). Novices may lack important knowledge or may have memorized a wealth of disconnected facts, without any organizing structure or concept to provide understanding or transfer to new situations. Because they do not yet have these organizers, they need rules to help them see the order of things and develop knowledge and schemata for future reference. Over time, as they become more proficient, some parts of the process no longer require conscious attention; they become automatic. When this happens, they can start to move outside rigorous adherence to the rules and begin to adapt and to make the learning their own, reflecting a unique constellation of talents and ideas. When something doesn't appear to be working, however, even experts go back to the rules as a strategy for self-monitoring and correction. Imagine a professional tennis player executing a serve. When it's working, it's an ace. When it's not, even a professional goes back to the practice court and to first principles, often with a video camera as an aid.

> The research . . . shows clearly that "usable knowledge" is not the same as a mere list of disconnected facts. Experts' knowledge is connected and organized around important concepts (e.g., Newton's second law of motion); it is "conditionalized" to specify the contexts in which it is applicable; it supports understanding and transfer (to other contexts) rather than only the ability to remember.
>
> —Brandsford et al. (1999)

Experts organize and classify their knowledge around important concepts and draw on these configurations of "usable knowledge" in their thinking because the ideas have become automatic parts of their thinking. With this kind of automaticity, experts can use the concepts in an unstructured world where there are complex interactions of multiple factors. They use metacognition and reflection to control and perfect their learning. Perhaps most important, they take personal responsibility for the outcomes of their learning, fine-tune their understanding by checking it against other information, and use self-monitoring to signal the need for a return to the rules or a search for new information.

As if it isn't complicated enough to think about making connections that stimulate "deep understanding," it is also important to remember that each individual is unique. As with all other human characteristics, learning is diverse and different for each learner. It is a function of heredity, experiences, perspectives, backgrounds, talents, interests, capacities, needs, and the unpredictable flow of any particular life. Learners have different emotional states, rates and styles of learning, stages of development, abilities, talents, feelings of efficacy, and needs. It is exactly this diversity that provides innumerable opportunities for expanding learning—first, by acknowledging differences in physiological, personal, linguistic, cultural, and social backgrounds, and second, by focusing on the common features that make all of us human. But the differences must be taken into account as well, to provide all learners with the necessary challenges and opportunities for learning and self-development.

Learning Is Hard Work

Living in dissonance and challenging "taken to be true" notions is hard work. People tend to strive for relative stability between their internal conceptions and new information and may even avoid conditions that disrupt the way they see the world. The challenge is to move beyond dissonance into productive learning. But what is it that compels people to live in the dissonance, experience the discomfort of not understanding something, and strive to integrate new knowledge, even when it requires serious adjustments to their prior beliefs? What motivates learning? Understanding how motivation works provides the key to keeping learning at the forefront and building patterns of learning that are automatic and last a lifetime.

Clearly, motivation to learn is more complicated than we thought. If learning is not primarily dependent on external rewards, what else influences it? And how does it work? According to motivational researchers, students are motivated by both success and competence. And they are influenced by their beliefs about what contributes to success. Students who believe that academic achievement is determined by fixed ability are more likely to work toward performance goals (i.e., grades) to please the teacher and appear competent. For these students, grades are the currency in school, and the exchange value of the grades is more important than the learning. Unfortunately, that means that they tend to pick easy tasks and are less likely to persist once they encounter difficulty (Stipek, 1996, cited in Shepard, 2000). Students who attribute academic success to their own efforts are more likely to adopt learning goals, which means they are motivated by an increasing sense of mastery and by the desire to become competent. When people succeed or fail, they explain their success or failure to themselves in various ways: effort, ability, task factors, or luck. Only the first of these attributions is likely to promote adaptive motivational tendencies. The student can decide to try harder and be successful. The other explanations—ability, task difficulty, or luck—are all out of the student's control. When students do not believe that they have control over their achievements, they are much less motivated to work in school.

Although motivation is an individual attribute, there are also dramatic cultural differences in the way teachers, parents, and students view the relative importance of ability and effort in their success. The relative emphasis that is given to ability and effort can have direct implications for the way people think about learning. Stevenson and Stigler (1992), in their book *The Learning Gap*, described a series of studies comparing American with Asian schools:

> In American society, learning tends to be regarded as an all-or-none process. A student who is "bright" is expected to just "get it," whereas duller students are assumed to lack the requisite ability for learning certain material. Under the "ability" model, motivation to try hard depends . . . a great deal on the individual child's assessment of whether s(he) has the ability to succeed. By contrast, the effort model, such as the Chinese and Japanese tend to hold, portrays learning as gradual and incremental, something that almost by definition must be acquired over a long period of time. (p. 102)

This difference in attitude, they believe, leads to a weakness in North American educational systems because of the pessimistic image that it offers most of our students. Stevenson and Stigler (1992) summarized their findings by saying,

> Ability models subvert learning through the effects they have on the goals that parents and teachers set for children and on

children's motivation to work hard to achieve these goals. Effort models offer a more hopeful alternative by providing a simple but effective formula for ensuring gradual change and improvement: "work hard and persist." (p. 106)

If motivation to learn is something that can be influenced, educators need to take a long, hard look at what they believe inspires students to learn.

The extent to which individuals see themselves as competent and capable has a dramatic effect on their willingness to attempt new learning (see Figure 4.2). People consciously or unconsciously ask questions such as, How uncomfortable will it make me? For how long?

When people consistently fail, they lose their motivation to learn and go to great lengths to avoid the pain of failure, the possibility of public humiliation, and additional confirmation of their incompetence. In essence, human beings deal with threat by down-shifting, turning off, and resisting engagement.

> Learning is a constructive process that occurs best when what is being learned is relevant and meaningful to the learner and when the learner is actively engaged in creating his or her own knowledge and understanding by connecting what is being learned with prior knowledge and experience.
>
> —Lambert and McCombs (1998)

Motivation also flags when someone succeeds too easily. There is no reason to continue to expend energy. Csikszentmihalyi (1990) explains that if a person has few skills and faces little challenge, he or she is apathetic, whereas if challenge is low but the skill level is higher, he or she is likely to experience boredom. When both levels of challenge and skill are high, he or she is in "flow." When people believe they are able to succeed, they are willing to try new and challenging tasks, even when such tasks are difficult. Therefore, continuous learning appears to depend on a combination of effort and obvious success. When students are in flow, as Csikszentmihalyi (1990) describes it, they are completely absorbed in the task at hand and will work hard and unflaggingly toward a goal, no matter how hard the new learning might be. The motivation for learning comes from achieving mastery of a skill or body of knowledge, and the initial passion can be the seed for higher levels of attainment.

On the other hand, if the work is boring and undemanding, or if the risk of failure and embarrassment is too high, young people quickly fill the time with activities they find more compelling, often to the chagrin of the adults around them.

Biggs and Moore (1993) talk about four broad categories of motivation, all of which can influence learning. *Extrinsic* motivation comes

Figure 4.2   Motivation as a Function of Challenge and Skill

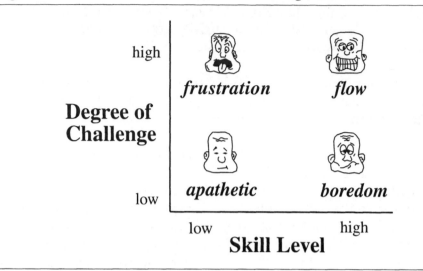

from outside and is central to surface learning. With extrinsic motivation, the task is carried out because it provides positive or negative reinforcing consequences. *Social* motivation is related to the influence of the person who formed the motive (i.e., parent, peer, or teacher) and the nature of the process (modeling, conformity, or cooperation) that he or she uses to engage the learner. *Achievement* motivation is what drives learning for the purpose of passing a test or getting a job. It is surface motivation, exemplified in actions such as rote learning, which may, nevertheless, produce academic success. *Intrinsic* motivation is internal and comes from a need to engage in learning for its own sake, with personal commitment.

For a long time, reinforcement and rewards have been considered important motivators. When initial interest in a task is low, rewards can increase the likelihood of academic engagement and performance of tasks. However, there is an interesting paradox about the nature and power of rewards when the behavior is intrinsically interesting. Extrinsic rewards have the potential to undermine performance, especially when the behaviors are ones that people are likely to do in the absence of the reward because they are inherently interested. There is a danger that when people who are highly intrinsically motivated are faced with a heavy accountability system of extrinsic rewards, they lose some of the intrinsic motivation and replace it with reinforcement from the reward. It is then very hard to return the behavior to the category of "important to do without a reward," and the behavior is likely to be less prevalent, not more.

As you can see, learning is not the exclusive purview of the intellect. It is also deeply emotional. As Daniel Goleman (1995) describes in his book *Emotional Intelligence,* thinking and rationality are the engine of our choices, but feelings and emotional intelligence help to streamline decisions by eliminating some options and highlighting others. It is the complementarity of feeling and thought that provides the balance to harmonize head and heart.

Learning, because it involves something new and unknown, inevitably triggers a range of emotions. New learning often includes a risk of failure and the possibility of discomfort and disorientation as the learner struggles to make sense of new ideas. As Goleman describes it, the body experiences an emotional hijacking, where surges in the limbic system capture the rest of the brain. This can result in a feeling of helplessness and a "down-shifting" to self-protective behaviors. It can also trigger flow, where the individual is totally and unself-consciously absorbed and engaged in the pleasure of the learning and doing (Csikszentmihalyi, 1990). Needless to say, people learn more and sustain their interest when they have experienced and are motivated by experiences of flow in their learning than when their learning is forced and the emotional response is fear and anxiety. This state of engagement is based on relaxed alertness, a combination of perceived safety and challenging learning experiences.

Learning Happens in Context

Learning doesn't take place in a vacuum, and learners are never tabula rasa (blank slates). They are not containers to be filled; rather, their minds are whirling, spiraling, dancing—connecting and challenging everything that they encounter in their social and physical environment. This process begins in tiny infants, and as they grow, they create coherent and (for them) reasonable patterns of the world around them. These beliefs about what the world is like come very early from interaction with the family and the community. Early experiential knowledge forms the fabric of children's lives and is often very resistant to change. It is the "stuff" that life has taught them. Learners test the veracity of their beliefs and their ideas (and those of their community and culture) by comparing them to the beliefs and ideas

> Learning occurs best in an environment that contains positive interpersonal relationships and interactions, comfort and order, and in which the learner feels appreciated, acknowledged, respected, and validated.
>
> —Lambert and McCombs (1998)

held by the people and the culture around them. This testing process often involves books, media, teachers, parents, and experts. Social interactions, formal and informal, are important contributors to learning and to the beliefs that people hold.

Vygotsky (1978) enhanced our understanding of learning as a social process. He argued that the capacity to learn from others is fundamental to human intelligence. With help from someone more knowledgeable or skilled, the learner is able to achieve more than he or she could achieve alone. Cooperation lies at the heart of success.

> Assumption: Learning in school is driven by what teachers and students do in classrooms.

Learning in schools, in particular, takes place in a social context. The nature of this social milieu has a profound effect on how, why, and what learning occurs. Classroom and school settings can be more or less learning friendly. One Australian study found that classrooms that are personalized encourage active participation, and the use of investigative skills produces more meaning-oriented approaches to learning in the students (Dart, Burnett, & Boulton-Lewis, 1999). People may also learn in one context but fail to transfer their learning to different contexts. When a subject is taught in many different contexts, however, and includes examples demonstrating broad applicability of what is taught, people are more likely to be able to abstract what is relevant and construct their own knowledge to apply flexibly as the situation arises. Perhaps most important, the learning context can influence learners' motivation and identities. Teachers' values and beliefs influence the type of structure they create in the classroom and their responses to students. Children are astute observers of teachers and can identify differential treatment by them (Weinstein, 1998), frequently lowering the motivation of students who see themselves as less able. Through detailed case studies of individual children throughout their primary schooling, Pollard and Filer (1999) demonstrate how they are continuously shaping, maintaining, and actively evolving their pupil identities as they move from one classroom context to the next. What this means is that each child's or young person's sense of self as a pupil can be enhanced or threatened by changes over time in their relationships, structural position in the classroom, and relative success or failure. It can also be affected by their teachers' expectations, learning and teaching strategies, classroom organization, and, as you will soon see, assessment and evaluation practices.

Ideas for Follow-Up

1. Use Figure 4.1 as an organizer for a mind map activity in which you identify things that you do (or could do) in your classroom assessment activities to capitalize on the human qualities identified by Costa.

2. Think of something you remember learning that is now automatic for you (e.g., a sport, driving a car). What was it like when you were learning it? What helped you get good at it?

CHAPTER 5

Assessment and Learning

As I mentioned in Chapter 3, Assessment *of* Learning is still the predominant approach to assessment in most schools, and the modes of choice are tests, essays, and projects. Even when teachers use informal assessments such as questioning in class and observing students, they typically do so to make or confirm judgments about individual students, and they rarely retain the information for very long or find a way of preserving it for future consideration.

In this book, I am proposing a major and fundamental shift in the way we think about assessment. Moving to a more equal place for Assessment *for* Learning and Assessment *as* Learning in the operation of schools and classrooms is a massive undertaking, but it is possible. Although Chapter 11 is dedicated to "getting there," the first step in this process is one of understanding and considering alternative views to the ones that have dominated our culture for so long.

In this chapter, I introduce the ideas, theory, and research that have led me and others to believe that assessment can and should be a key part of learning. Why do we think that classroom assessment is so important? How can classroom assessment be linked to learning? If classroom assessment can be that powerful, how does it work?

> Never doubt that a small group of thoughtful, committed citizens can change the world; indeed, it's the only thing that ever has.
>
> —Margaret Mead

How Does Assessment Contribute to Learning?

Classroom assessment will always have an impact of some kind on students and their learning. It is the basis for decisions that teachers make about things like what to teach and to whom, what to communicate to parents, and promotion to the next grade. It is the basis for decisions that students make as well—about such things as their sense of personal accomplishment, their feelings of self-worth, and their willingness to engage in the academic work of schools. It defines consolidation of learning and affects the development of enduring learning strategies and skills. Ultimately, it influences the value that students attach to educa-

tion. If assessment has this kind of impact, it deserves careful attention so that it supports learning rather than hampering it.

> Assessment that is explicitly designed to promote learning is the single most powerful tool we have for raising standards and empowering life long learning.
>
> —Assessment Reform Group (1999)

Just doing classroom assessment doesn't necessarily contribute to learning, however. Remember, most classroom assessment is summative Assessment *of* Learning. Even more child-centered approaches using performance assessments, portfolios, or records of achievement are only a small step toward using assessment that really encourages students to progress.

Researchers studying classroom assessment have found that formative assessment can contribute to learning. In 1988, the *Review of Educational Research* published a comprehensive review of literature about the impact of classroom assessment practices on students done by Terry Crooks, from New Zealand. He made a strong, research-based case that classroom assessment has both short- and long-term effects on learning. In the short term, classroom assessment can

- Focus attention on important aspects of the subject
- Give students opportunities to practice skills and consolidate learning
- Guide further instructional or learning activities.

In the medium and long term, assessment holds the possibility of

- Influencing students' motivation as learners and their perceptions of their capabilities
- Communicating and reinforcing teaching goals, including performance criteria and desired standards of performance
- Influencing students' choice of and development of learning strategies, skills, and study patterns
- Influencing students' subsequent choice of courses, activities, and careers (Crooks, 1988).

In the United States, people such as Walt Haney and George Madaus (1989), Lorrie Shepard (1989), Grant Wiggins (1989), and Rick Stiggins (1991) were proposing that we needed better assessments and that classroom assessment held the key to learning for students.

A decade later, Paul Black and Dylan Wiliam (1998), in England, synthesized evidence from more than 250 studies linking assessment and learning. The Assessment Reform Group (1999), also in England, described their finding as follows:

> The outcome was a clear and incontrovertible message: that initiatives designed to enhance effectiveness of the way assessment is used in the classroom to promote learning can raise pupil attainment. (p. 4)

This review reinforced the potential of classroom assessment. The authors indicated that classroom assessment that promotes learning

- Is embedded as an essential part of teachers' views of teaching or learning
- Involves sharing learning goals with students
- Aims to help students to know and to recognize the standards they are aiming for
- Involves students in self-assessment
- Provides feedback which leads to students recognizing their next steps and how to take them
- Is underpinned by confidence that every student can improve
- Involves both teachers and pupils reflecting on assessment data. (Assessment Reform Group, 1999, p. 7)

Black and Wiliam (1998) also identified several inhibiting factors:

- Teachers' tendency to assess quantity of work and presentation, rather than quality of learning
- Greater attention given to marking and grading, much of it tending to lower the self-esteem of students, rather than to providing advice for improvement
- A strong emphasis on comparing students with each other, which demoralizes the less successful students
- Teachers' feedback to students serving social and managerial purposes rather than helping them to learn more effectively
- Teachers not knowing enough about their students' learning needs

Using assessment practices to add to learning is clearly a complex undertaking. It means paying attention to student engagement and motivation. It means making connections, referring to progressions of learning and to learning goals, and planning relationships and linkages between instruction and assessment. It means thinking about students individually as well as collectively. It means reinforcing important ideas, identifying gaps or misconceptions, and building on students' beliefs to steer them toward clear understanding.

This Is Not Just About Assessment

It is obvious that assessment is not everything. But it should also be clear that teaching without assessment as an integral part of the process is also not enough. Rethinking assessment is one small part of boosting the quality of teaching and learning in schools. Classrooms where assessment is viewed as an integral part of learning are very different from other classrooms. Teachers who are working with a new view of assessment as part of learning are finding that it isn't possible to change assessment and leave everything else the same. When assessment changes, so does teaching, so does classroom organization, and so does interaction with students and parents.

The biggest change that I can foresee in changing the balance of the links between assessment and instruction is a fundamental power shift. Assessment as learning requires

> Assumption: Assessment and learning are intimately intertwined and often indistinguishable from one another.

the involvement of both students and parents. It is not a private activity for teachers, and certainly not a process that governments can control. It is a personal, iterative, and evolving conversation in which teachers are assessing and describing performance in ways that are useful to others, who will make their own decisions about what to do next.

In the following chapters, I have used examples from both colleagues and graduate students with whom I have worked that highlight occasions when assessment was designed to enhance students' learning. Although I have organized the material into separate chapters, using the examples to highlight particular ideas, each of them offers a range of insights into the role of assessment. They all represent integrated, whole, and thoughtfully prepared approaches to assessment that have learning as the goal. Taken together, they give a range of examples of what good assessment looks like.

Ideas for Follow-Up

1. What have you read in this chapter that reinforces beliefs that you hold already? What has challenged your beliefs?

2. What are the barriers in schools to using assessment as learning?

CHAPTER  6

Using Assessment to Identify What Students Believe to Be True

As I described in Chapter 4, learning is an interactive process by which learners try to make sense of new information and integrate it into what they already know. Students are always thinking, and they are either challenging or reinforcing their thinking on a moment-by-moment basis. Before teachers can plan for targeted teaching and classroom activities, they need to have a sense of what it is that students are thinking. What is it that they believe to be true? This process involves much more than, "Do they have the right or wrong answer?" It means making students' thinking visible and understanding the images and patterns that they have constructed in order to make sense of the world from their perspective.

The choice of assessment task is a critical feature if it is going to help the teacher see the students' thinking. It has to provide the opportunity for the students to deploy the knowledge and skills that the teacher is trying to investigate, from a variety of points of view. Teachers need detailed images so that they can foresee the possible responses of the students, a feat of imaginative prediction that demands considerable expertise (Black, 1998).

"The Case of the Pool Table"

At the beginning of the school year, a middle school mathematics teacher uses a series of games that he has devised to give him insights into his students' knowledge and depth of understanding of concepts in the mathematics curriculum. One of these games uses a modified pool table to help him ascertain the students' conceptions of algebraic relationships, either

Figure 6.1   The Pool Table Task

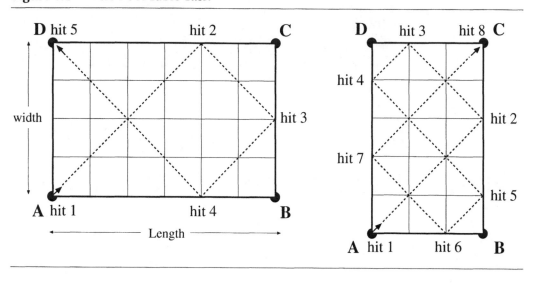

formally or intuitively. Students in a Grade 7/8 mathematics class were given a graphic of a four-pocket pool table (see Figure 6.1).[1]

The students were told that the ball always leaves Pocket A at a 45° angle, rebounds off a wall at an equal angle to that at which the wall was struck, and continues until it ends up in a pocket. Students counted the number of squares through which the ball passed, as well as the number of hits the ball made, the first and last hit being the starting and finishing pockets. They experimented with tables of various dimensions and recorded their observations on a chart (see Table 6.1).

As the students gathered data (with many more data combinations than I have included in the table), they began to make predictions about the number of hits, the number of squares, and the destination of the ball, based on the patterns that they observed. Some moved to general statements of relationships, such as, "You can tell the number of hits by adding the width and the length together and dividing by their greatest common factor," or "The number of squares that the ball goes through is always the lowest common multiple of the width and

Table 6.1   Recordkeeping of Hits (Pool Table Task)

Length	Width	Number of Hits	Number of Squares
6	4	5	12
3	5	8	15
5	4		
3	2		
8	4		

the length." Other students continued to count to reach the answers without seeing the relationships that existed.

During this task, the teacher wandered around the room observing and noting the thinking that was occurring for individual students. He stopped and asked questions, not about the answers that they were recording but about the process that they were using. He prompted students to think about the patterns and to take a chance at making predictions. All the while, he was making notes on a scratch pad that contained the names of the students and blank fields for writing his observations. From this information, he decided how to proceed in teaching the next series of lessons and how to group the students for the various instructional elements to come. For some, the work progressed quickly to an introduction of formal notation of an algebraic equation to symbolize the general patterns that they had identified. For others, the teacher used a number of patterning exercises to help them see the patterns that arose and formulate them in concrete ways. He was conscious of the importance of moving from concrete experience and direct consciousness of the phenomenon to the more abstract representation. The pool table task gave him a window into the students' thinking and a starting place for planning instruction, resources, grouping, timing, and pacing. When he moves on to another concept, all of these are likely to change. Once again, he needed to see what the students see, what they think, and what they understand before he could decide what he was going to do.

Start With What Students Believe to Be True

Students come to school with preconceptions about the way the world works. If their initial understanding is not engaged, they may fail to grasp new concepts and information or may memorize material for the immediate purposes (e.g., the test) but revert to their preconceptions outside the classroom. Often, these preconceptions include stereotypes and simplifications. Nevertheless, they have a profound effect on the integration of new concepts and information. Unless teachers really figure out what students believe is true and confront their notions about the world, they will continue to hold onto many misconceptions, some of which will make it impossible for them ever to truly understand more complex phenomena that build on this prior knowledge.

Assessment is the window into students' preconceptions, a way of finding out not just what they know, but what they believe to be true. Teachers need an accurate grasp of what students (individually and collectively) believe to be true in order to use this knowledge as a starting point for teaching, all the while monitoring their changing conceptions and altering teaching to fit. Errors are the window into students' learning. Understanding students' incomplete understandings, false beliefs, misconceptions, and naïve interpretations of concepts gives teachers some clues for creating conditions for learning. These preconceptions must be addressed before any new learning can take place, particularly if they are inconsistent with the new knowledge and the learner must accommodate to the new information by changing beliefs. Unless the teacher can figure out what students believe and what would convince them that their ideas are flawed or simplistic, students will continue to hold on to their preconceptions.

Teachers need constant information about what students know and the strategies being used to process and comprehend new concepts. By embedding diagnostic assessment in instructional activities, teachers can preserve the integrity of assessment tasks and protect instructional time that would otherwise be diverted (Shepard, 1989). They can also get closer to the images that students hold.

"The Case of the Bog"

In a local school district, all students in Grade 8 participated in a writing assessment based on a real decision by the city to build a new school on fragile land. Table 6.2 shows the task for the students.

The district used the rubric in Table 6.3 to assess the students' performance. This typical scoring strategy satisfied the district's accountability needs and also provided district curriculum consultants and teachers with insights about the dimensions of written language that needed attention in elementary schools.

One teacher, who happened also to be a talented graduate student, took the process further. She believes that teachers need to unpack the process of writing in order to help their students move forward. For her, the information in this rubric was useful, but it wasn't enough to allow her to understand what students needed next. She used the Cognitive Domain of the Taxonomy of Educational Objectives (Gronlund, 2000) and Core Thinking Skills (Marzano et al., 1988) to devise a mechanism for considering the students' responses in relation to their learning (and teaching) needs. Table 6.4 is the combined organizer that she created.

By using this framework for the analysis, she could gain additional insights into how the students are thinking and what teachers can do to help them improve. Imagine a group of teachers receiving student papers from the assessment and collectively reviewing those papers as a way of making detailed diagnostic notes about each student as a

Table 6.2   The Bog Task

Background Information	Recently, the City of XXX and the District School Board have been debating a proposal for the construction of a new elementary school, Sherwood Mills Public School. The proposed school site is adjacent to the XXX Bog, which has been the habitat of many wetland creatures for the past century. The controversy centers on the need for the new school and the preservation of the wetlands. You will be asked to do the following:
Description of the Task	• Collect data about both the conditions of the XXX Bog and the need for a community school in that area. • Identify the main problems. • Form an opinion as to whether or not the school board should go ahead with the construction of the Sherwood Mills School. • Substantiate your opinion by creating diagrams, graphs, or maps to support your point of view. Include personal experiences to enrich your argument. • Make recommendations about the building proposal. Validate your answer. • Draft an article that includes your opinion, your supporting reasons, and your recommendations regarding the proposed building. • Refine your draft, and make sure to include a powerful concluding statement of your point of view.

starting point for planning the next term and ensuring that students received the assistance that they needed. I have included just one student paper (with a pseudonym, of course) to illustrate what they can learn. Jonathon's report is displayed in Table 6.5.

In a joint planning session, a group of teachers analyzed Jonathon's responses to the questions and his final report using the District Writing Scales and the more detailed consideration of his thinking (see Table 6.6).

Table 6.7 gives their observations of gaps based on the framework described above.

On the basis of their analysis, the teachers made a number of suggestions for Jonathon's teacher. These are displayed in Table 6.8.

(Text continues on page 66)

Table 6.3   District Writing Rubric

Grade 8 Performance Assessment . . . the Bog

Trait/Level	1	2	3	4
Voice	• Not successful in capturing attention • Text lacks sincerity • Little or no evidence of tone	• Not very successful in capturing and maintaining attention • Text not very convincing and sincere • Minimal tone	• Fairly successful in capturing attention • Text somewhat convincing and sincere • Tone is fairly effective, i.e., creates mood	• Successful in capturing and maintaining attention • Text convincing and sincere • Tone effective, i.e., creates mood
Organization	• Minimal logical plan and sequence interferes with comprehension • No clear intro and/or conclusion • Transitions are omitted • Paragraphs: no evidence	• Overall logical plan and sequence present but weak • Intro and/or conclusion weak • Transitions are not always used • Paragraphs are sparse	• Adequate overall logical plan and sequence • Intro and conclusion are adequate and related • Transitions are used where needed • Paragraphs may not appear throughout entire text	• Very good overall logical plan and sequence • Intro and conclusion are strong and effective • Transitions are used appropriately and skillfully • Paragraphs at appropriate times
Ideas & Content	• Unclear main idea/purpose • Text wanders • Simplistic • Inaccuracies in info	• Main idea/ purpose recognizable • Focus somewhat flawed • Predictable	• Main idea/ purpose reasonably clear • Text shows focus, some lapses • Fairly interesting	• Very clear main idea/ purpose • Text focused • Interesting, original, insightful

(Continued)

Table 6.3 (*Continued*)

Grade 8 Performance Assessment . . . the Bog

Trait/Level	1	2	3	4
(*Ideas & Content, continued*)	• Poorly blended from source	• Supporting details repetitive, unrelated • Not well blended from source	• Supporting details fairly accurate • Fairly well blended from source	• Supporting details accurate • Well blended from source
Conventions	• Weak command of grade-appropriate conventions • Minimal command of advanced conventions	• Fair command of grade-appropriate conventions • Inconsistent command of advanced conventions	• Good command of grade-appropriate conventions • Fair command of advanced conventions	• Excellent command of grade-appropriate conventions • Good command of advanced conventions
Effective Use of Language	• Many lapses in fluency • No variation in sentence length/structure • Word choice is limited • Figurative language rarely used	• Some lapses in fluency • Little variation in sentence length/structure • Word choice somewhat limited • Figurative language used occasionally	• Fairly fluent, smooth, and natural • Some sentences vary in length/structure • Word choice is generally appropriate • Figurative language used fairly successfully	• Fluent, smooth, and natural • Sentences vary in length/structure • Word choice is appropriate • Figurative language used successfully

Table 6.4   Links Between the Bog Task and the Cognitive Domain of the Taxonomy of Educational Objectives (Gronlund, 2000) and the Core Thinking Skills (Marzano et al., 1988)

Question on the Bog Task	Cognitive Domain Categories (Gronlund, 2000) Required for This Question	Core Thinking Skills (Marzano et al., 1988) Required for This Question
1. Collect data about both the conditions of the XXX Bog and the need for a community school in that area.	Knowledge: Remembering previously learned material • Recall of information pertinent to environmental issues (including appropriate vocabulary) • Able to identify, define, describe facts pertinent to environmental issues Comprehension: Grasps the meaning of material • Identification of the main problem • Shows comprehension of facts and principles by summarizing, sequencing, generalizing, inferring, explaining, and extending facts presented in reading materials and discussions	Information gathering: Obtaining information through observation and formulating questions by clarifying issues and meaning through inquiry • Remembering: activities and strategies used to retrieve pertinent information • Activating prior knowledge regarding environmental and/or wetland issues Organizing skills: Used to arrange information so that it can be understood or presented effectively • Comparing and identifying similarities and differences, and classifying this information so that it makes sense and student can make personal links with information
2. Identify the main problem	Comprehension: Grasps the meaning of material • Shows comprehension of facts and principles by paraphrasing, predicting, and inferring • Can estimate future consequences implied in the reading material, data, websites, etc.	Analyzing skills: Clarifying existing information by examining parts and relationships • Identifying the key components regarding the issue of building on an environmentally sensitive piece of land vs. building a community school

(Continued)

Table 6.4 *(Continued)*

Question on the Bog Task	*Cognitive Domain Categories (Gronlund, 2000) Required for This Question*	*Core Thinking Skills (Marzano et al., 1988) Required for This Question*
		• Identify main ideas Focusing skills: Defining problems in order to clarify puzzling situations • What is the statement of the problem? • Who has the problem? What makes it a problem? • Give examples
3. and 4. Form an opinion about whether or not XXX District School Board should go ahead with the construction of Sherwood Mills School. Substantiate your opinion through the use of diagrams, graphs, or maps to support your point of view. Include personal experiences to enrich your argument.	Application: Use learned material in new and concrete situations • Applies concepts and principles to new situations • Makes predictions about cause and effect Analysis: Break down material into its component parts so that its organizational structure becomes apparent • Recognizes logical fallacies in reasoning • Distinguishes between facts and fiction • Evaluates the relevance of available information and/or data Synthesis: Put parts together to create a new whole • Draws conclusions through gathering information from varied and reliable sources	Analyzing skills: Clarifying existing information by examining parts and relationships • Identify relationships and patterns from discussions, key articles, primary and secondary sources Generating and integrating skills: Use of prior knowledge to add information beyond primary and secondary sources • Experiential and/or personal links • Makes inferences due to inductive (making generalizations and logical statements based on observation or analysis of various cases) or deductive reasoning (ability to extend an existing principle or idea in a logical manner)

(Continued)

Table 6.4 *(Continued)*

Question on the Bog Task	Cognitive Domain Categories (Gronlund, 2000) Required for This Question	Core Thinking Skills (Marzano et al., 1988) Required for This Question
	• Integrates learning from different constructs into a plan for solving a problem	• Anticipation of an outcome (predicting) based upon prior knowledge, discussions in class, reading materials, etc. • Adding details, explanations, examples, or other relevant information to support and/or improve understanding (elaboration) . . . indicates that student is able to relate the new information to prior experiences and/or knowledge
5. Think of any recommendations that you would make about this building proposal. Validate your answer.	Synthesis: Put parts together to create a new whole, with an emphasis on the creation of new patterns or structures • Draws conclusions through gathering information from varied and reliable sources • Integrates learning from different constructs into a plan for solving a problem • Categorizes, compiles, reconstructs, relates, reorganizes, revises, rewrites, or summarizes information pertinent to the topic and/or opinion Evaluation: Judge the value of materials for a given purpose, with the	Analyzing skills: Clarifying existing information by examining parts and relationships Integrating skills: Ability to put together the relevant pieces of a solution • New information and prior knowledge connected to make meaningful connections Evaluation skills: Being able to assess the reasonableness and quality of ideas • Verification of ideas; ability to confirm or prove the truth of an idea based upon reliable primary sources of information

(Continued)

Table 6.4 *(Continued)*

Question on the Bog Task	Cognitive Domain Categories (Gronlund, 2000) Required for This Question	Core Thinking Skills (Marzano et al., 1988) Required for This Question
	judgments determined by a set of criteria (either predetermined or gathered independently) • Appraises, compares, concludes, contrasts, describes, discriminates, interprets, or justifies pertinent information to form an opinion with validating evidence	
6. Draft an article that includes your opinion, your supporting reasons, and your recommendations regarding the proposed building of Sherwood Mills School.	Synthesis: Put parts together to create a new whole, with an emphasis on the creation of new patterns or structures • Draws conclusions through gathering information from varied and reliable sources • Integrates learning from different constructs into a plan for solving a problem • Categorizes, compiles, reconstructs, relates, reorganizes, revises, rewrites, or summarizes information pertinent to the topic and/or opinion Evaluation: Judge the value of materials for a given purpose, with the judgments determined by a set of criteria (either	Integrating skills: Ability to put together the relevant pieces of a solution Evaluation skills: Being able to assess the reasonableness and quality of ideas • Establishing criteria … being able to set standards for judging the value or logic of ideas • Checking the accuracy of facts through several reliable sources Integrating skills: Ability to put together the relevant pieces of a solution • Restructuring; bringing in new information that might challenge old beliefs, concepts … student actively modifies, extends, recognizes that previously held beliefs might be flawed or valid

Table 6.4 *(Continued)*

Question on the Bog Task	Cognitive Domain Categories (Gronlund, 2000) Required for This Question	Core Thinking Skills (Marzano et al., 1988) Required for This Question
	predetermined or gathered independently) • Appraises, compares, concludes, contrasts, describes, discriminates, interprets, or justifies pertinent information to form an opinion with validating evidence	
7. Refine your draft and be sure to include a powerful concluding statement pertaining to your point of view.	Synthesis: Put parts together to create a new whole, with an emphasis on the creation of new patterns or structures • Draws conclusions through gathering information from varied and reliable sources • Integrates learning from different constructs into a plan for solving a problem • Categorizes, compiles, reconstructs, relates, reorganizes, revises, rewrites, or summarizes information pertinent to the topic and/or opinion	Integrating skills: Ability to put together the relevant pieces of a solution • Ability to summarize information

SOURCE: Created by Mary Lou McKinley, doctoral student, OISE/UT, as part of her thesis, "Using the Analysis of a Performance-Based Writing Task to Address the Gaps in Student Learning and to Suggest Teaching Strategies for Teachers of Young Adolescents."

Table 6.5   Jonathon's Report

Final Draft Of Article   April 9th 1999

The city of _____, and the _____ District School Board, have been debating the proposal of a new elementary school. The elementary school's site is to be on the _____ wetlands site, which is home to very rare, flora and fauna, and has been for the past century. This decision will be based on the need for the new __ school, and the preservation of the _____ wetlands.

I am strongly against the proposal to build this new school where the wetlands stand. The bog should be preserved for natural history. It holds quiet a bit of geological history. It Carbondates to a melting glacier some 12,000 years ago. Also, it is home for a lot of very rare flora and fauna, which cannot be found in any other place in Ontario and

The _____ wetlands existed from the time of mammoth's and mastodons, with being the only _____ location for over 21 native plants and other species, It is like an outdoor museum and it is educational for present and future generations. Also it is a "priceless legacy".

The _____ wetlands is a high quality habitat and one of only two provincially significant wetlands in the city of _____.

The wetlands are significant due to the rarity in its region. Proof of its significance is that it is the only place in _____ which has gooseberry bushes, Tamaracks and mud plat. It is also home to the Northern Harrier and the Short-eared Owl.

(Continued)

Table 6.5 (*Continued*)

The bog is 12,000 years old, Paul Maycock, a botany at _____ College, says to have "the mud to prove it".

James Bradley, an Environment minister, proposed that it could be a "three way participation" which would result to preserving the wetlands and the buffer zone.

Gary Gallon, who is an assitant of James Bradley, says the cost of bringing property into public hands, would be alot less than the original cost of $54 million dollars.

Dr. McAndrew's, who is a proffesor of botany and geology, and the curator of botany for the Royal Ontario Museum, says that a lot of questions can be answered by the study of the wetlands. Beth Bremner and Herb Ruch say that the wetlands are "unbelivably unique", they also said that "they benifit to science, schools and public is truly obvious".

The CVCA want the rare flora and fauna to be re-examined and re-evaluated. The citizen's committee recommend a "mediator". Local politicians should wist the bag before making a final

decision. There should be a re-evaluation based on information from a botanist. It could go to the OMB for final agreement seeing as it is taking over 10 years to make a decision. Local support from the community could make a difference. Arranging a land swap could work out as well.

The _____ wetlands should be preserved for educational Reasons. It is very interesting to have all the rare flora and fauna to learn about, and we need some kind of natural resource in our city, rather than buildings and what not.

Table 6.6   Jonathon's Scores and the Rationale Using the District
Writing Scale

XXX District Writing Scales and Student's Score	*Rationale for Score*	*Examples From Student's Paper*
Voice 2+	• Fairly successful in capturing attention • Attempt made to persuade, but text is very routine & not convincing • Minimal level of tone is evident . . . only slightly effective in evoking reader response (e.g., increase in knowledge, understanding, insight, opinion/ attitude change)	"I am strongly against the proposal for a new school where the wetlands stand. The bog should be preserved for natural history. It holds quiet a bit of geological history . . . home for rare flora and fauna . . ."
Organization 2+	• Paragraphs do appear throughout text but occasionally run together or begin in the wrong places • Transitions not evident • Some evidence of structure (rambles at times) • Intro & conclusion recognizable but weak & not entirely related • Intro is simply a reorganization of the original question	"The city of XXX, and the XXX District School Board, have been debating the proposal of a new elementary school. . . . decision will be based on the need for a new school, and the preservation of the XXX wetlands." (intro) "The XXX wetlands should be preserved for educational reasons. It is very interesting to have all the flora and fauna . . . rather than buildings and what not."
Ideas and Content 2	• Some facts presented but argument not focused • Writer generally stays on topic but does not develop a clear theme	"I am strongly against the proposal to build this new school . . . Paul Maycoct, a botany at XXX College, says to have 'the mud to prove

(Continued)

Table 6.6 (*Continued*)

XXX District Writing Scales and Student's Score	Rationale for Score	Examples From Student's Paper
	• Paper states opinion but does not expand or give reasons to support the opinion nor develop the opinion with further explanation (personal experiences and/or readings) • Facts presented in isolation . . . not always related to stated opinion • Does not contain reference to opposite point of view • Paper includes numerous pieces of information from assigned reading materials but not well blended from sources • Attempt made to relate some of the information, but relationship not clearly established because ideas are incomplete and underdeveloped (amount of explanation is limited)	it.' James Bradley, an Environment minister, proposed that it could be a 'three way participation' which would result in preserving the wetland and the buffer zone . . ." "Beth Bremmer and Herb Ruch say that the wetland are 'unbelievably unique,' they also said that 'they benefit to science, schools and publish is truly obvious.'"
Conventions 3-	• Fairly good command of grade-appropriate spelling, punctuation, and grammar conventions (a bit of difficulty with homonyms) • Some inconsistency of more advanced conventions—	"The elementary school's site . . . holds quiet a bit of geological history."

(*Continued*)

Table 6.6 (*Continued*)

XXX District Writing Scales and Student's Score	*Rationale for Score*	*Examples From Student's Paper*
	e.g., correct use of the possessive; using a wide variety of subordinate clauses; etc. • Minimal-to-moderate revision/correction of conventions required	
Effective Use of Language *2*	• Text is fairly smooth but sometimes tends to show lapses in fluency • Vocabulary & choice of words directly from reading materials but sometimes used awkwardly and/or inappropriately when transferred to own work	"The CVCV want the rare flora and fauna to be re-examined and re-evaluation. The citizen's committee recommend a 'mediator.' Local politicians should visit the bog before making a final decision. There should be a re-evaluation based on information from a botanist. It could go to the OMB for final agreement seeing as it is taking over 10 years to make a decision. Vocal support from the community could make a difference. Arranging a land swap could work out as well . . ."

Table 6.7   Gaps Identified Based on Detailed Analysis of "The Bog" Task for Jonathon Smith

---

Gaps in Student Learning . . . Derived From the Criterion-Referenced Scale

Organization

- Some evidence of structure (rambles at times)
- Intro & conclusion recognizable but weak & not entirely related
- Intro is simply a reorganization of the original question

Ideas and Content

- Some facts presented but argument not focused
- Writer generally stays on topic but does not develop a clear theme
- Paper states opinion but does not expand or give reasons to support the opinion nor develop the opinion with further explanation (personal experiences and/or readings)
- Facts presented in isolation . . . not always related to stated opinion
- Does not contain reference to opposite point of view
- Paper includes numerous pieces of information from assigned reading materials but not well blended from sources
- Attempt made to relate some of the information, but relationship not clearly established because ideas are incomplete and underdeveloped (amount of explanation is limited)

Effective Use of Language

- Text is fairly smooth but sometimes tends to show lapses in fluency
- Vocabulary & choice of words directly from reading materials but sometimes used awkwardly and/or inappropriately when transferred to own work

Gaps in Student Learning . . . Links to the Bog Task

- Difficulties in collecting information with regards to the issues of preserving a unique environmental area and the need for building a school in a high growth area
- Question as to whether there are gaps in student's understanding of wetlands, environmental issues, etc. (prior knowledge)
- Appeared to have difficulties in identifying main problem
- Stated an opinion . . . supported this opinion with random statement from the readings provided . . . no links to personal experiences
- Opinion not substantiated
- No recommendations given . . . references to reading materials but no specific recommendations given as to why building on the wetlands should not be supported

---

(Continued)

Table 6.7 (*Continued*)

Gaps in Student Learning . . . Links to Cognitive Domain & Core Thinking Skills (Gronlund, 2000; Marzano et al., 1988)

- Difficulties in recalling, explaining, extending facts pertaining to environmental issues . . . no experiential or personal links (knowledge, comprehension, Gronlund, 2000; information gathering, organizing skills, Marzano et al., 1988)
- Difficulties in grasping the meaning of the materials presented and blending the sources as supporting evidence in order to identify the main problem (comprehension, Gronlund, 2000; analyzing skills, focusing skills, Marzano et al., 1988)
- Stated a definite opinion but appeared to have difficulties in supporting opinion from available sources . . . facts presented in isolation and not well blended from sources (analyzing skills, generating and integrating skills, Marzano et al., 1988; analysis, Gronlund, 2000)
- Difficulties in identifying relationships and patterns from discussions and key articles (application, Gronlund, 2000; generating and integrating skills, Marzano et al., 1988)
- Difficulties in putting together relevant information (prior knowledge and new information) to make meaningful connections (evaluation and synthesis, Gronlund, 2000; analyzing skills, evaluation skills, integrating skills, Marzano et al., 1988)

Table 6.8　Suggestions for Next Steps in Instruction With Jonathon

- Activation of prior knowledge using a graphic organizer (Know, Want to Know, Learned) to establish what the student knows or believes to be true
- Instruction on how to connect prior knowledge to new information . . . right-angled thinking
- Identification of critical terms and phrases used in a variety of different situations with emphasis on those terms that are pertinent to the topic being discussed—for example, a "naturally preserved, historical site"— through explicit teaching during discussion of reading materials
- Instruction about how to use pertinent facts to support a stated opinion. Teaching that facts

  - Are specific to the informational content
  - Convey information about issues pertaining to people, places
  - Relate to the argument

- Instruction in how to use cause/effect sequences to consolidate students' understanding about how fragile an ecosystem can be and the impact of changing the natural habitat

Once again, in this example, assessment, curriculum targets, planning, and instruction are seamless. The process is dynamic, and the teachers move from one to the next effortlessly, with a focus on identifying what they know already, what they need to know, and what his teacher can do to support Jonathon's learning.

Ideas for Follow-Up

Analyze assessment tasks that you use already to identify the prerequisite learnings embedded in the tasks. Look at student papers to identify the places where they have misconceptions or lack the prerequisite knowledge to do the task. What instructional strategies could you use to scaffold their learning?

Note

1. This task was first described in Katz (1999).

Using Assessment to Motivate Learning

Motivation has always been a central factor in learning, as I described in Chapter 4. Simply put, motivation affects the amount of time and energy students are willing to devote to any task. Much of what we currently know about motivation to learn, however, is contrary to the folk wisdom of the past. Our view of motivation has been heavily influenced by the behaviorist psychology of the 1960s and 1970s. This theory describes how schedules of rewards and punishments lead to behavior being either reinforced or extinguished. In schools, this theory has been translated into practices of encouraging academically productive behavior with rewards and eliminating academically nonproductive behavior through punishment. This theory is deeply embedded in the way classrooms operate and has become almost an unquestioned "truth." Assessment has been the mechanism for doling out rewards and punishments in the form of grades (Stiggins, 2001). Marks have been cast as the ultimate motivator, but researchers have found that the relationship between marks and motivation is neither simple nor predictable. Marks have been found to be motivating for some students and demotivating for others (Stiggins, 1997). Students who generally do well often will be motivated by the likelihood of success and praise that accompanies doing well again. Students who typically do not do well may choose to avoid the likelihood of a failure experience by devaluing the assessment process and even devaluing school. What could be worse than failing a test? My guess would be working hard to pass

> The assessments that drive student learning and academic self-worth are those used in classrooms.
>
> —Stiggins (1990)

and still failing the test. If the student doesn't exert any effort, he or she can at least save face.

Assessment That Motivates

Motivation is essential for the hard work of learning. Even when students find the content interesting and the activity enjoyable, learning requires sustained concentration and effort. The cognitive demand of any new learning is a cost that has to be offset. Assessment can be a motivator, not through rewards or punishment, but by stimulating the intrinsic interest of students and providing them with the direction and confidence that they need to take the risk. When they don't have the tools or the capacities to reach the goals, the students have fallen through thin ice; without the strength to kick themselves out, they simply hang on with their fingertips, waiting to be rescued. Increasing capacity and fostering learning need to build both confidence and competence through early victories and a sense that the vision is doable in increments (Wiggins, 1998). Assessment can contribute to this process and enhance motivation by being relevant, appealing to students' imagination, and providing the scaffolding that they need to genuinely succeed.

Relevant Assessment

When assessment capitalizes on students' interests, enthusiasm, and talents and provides images of the world that lies ahead of them, it is much more likely to engage and inspire them so that the learning is itself the motivator. By making connections between curriculum, instruction, assessment, and students' daily lives—whether through looking at today's parallels for King Lear's behavior or comparing Mozart's life with that of a current popular composer—teachers can engage students and draw them into the learning that assessment encompasses. Assessment does not stand apart; rather, it is interwoven with teaching and learning to make connections for students, reinforcing what they know and challenging their thinking.

Imaginative Assessment

Children have vivid imaginations that allow them to see many possibilities in their minds that aren't available to them in real life. Assessment that is open-ended and allows for a range of solutions and approaches can capitalize on this natural interest and passion to engage students in reasoning critically, solving complex problems, and applying their knowledge in making novel connections between disparate things or seeing things in ways that might be missed otherwise. As less and less of what we thought was known remains stable and unchallenged, imagination may well be a critical faculty for students as they confront the world as it really is—a whole series of messy, seemingly insoluble problems to unravel, explore, and try to solve.

Assessment That Scaffolds Learning

Students are very aware that they are likely to face challenges and the unknown in their futures. They need to be confident that they can handle whatever they encounter. And they learn best when they are in a context that provides moderate challenge. When the task is too difficult, students may feel threatened and become self-protective. When the task is too simple, students may coast into inattention and boredom (Jensen, 1998). A task is appropriately challenging when students are expected to risk and move into the unknown, but they know how to get started and have support for reaching the new level of learning. This is what Vygotsky (1930/1978) called the "zone of proximal development"—that zone of competence that learners can navigate with support and that they are able to negotiate successfully with reasonable effort. In this zone, students get stuck but have the skills to consider various options and get themselves unstuck.

Assessment can be the vehicle that keeps new learning from being so obscure, difficult, or complicated that most students lose interest or find it impenetrable. Motivation is enhanced when errors and mistakes are treated as a normal part of learning, with timely feedback and a chance to rethink and redo the work, and when assessment is designed to provide students with access to their progress and allows them to stay engaged with the task. When assessment is designed to give students and teachers insight into what they are able to do independently as well as with guidance, students are empowered to seek help and the teacher is able to provide assistance at the point of learning, not at the end of instruction. When teachers intervene during learning, they can provide opportunities to see, imitate, and try out complex skills under their guidance. This kind of assessment has to occur in the middle of teaching and learning. It can (and should be) idiosyncratic and targeted. Why? Because it creates the perfect opportunity for teachers to teach exactly what students need to know and to provide focused feedback to move their learning forward. Sometimes, it even fosters flow—the kind of engagement in a task that is so focused and so absorbing that everything else disappears (Csikszentmihalyi, 1990).

"The Case of *Othello*"

To the chagrin of most English teachers, Shakespeare's plays are often viewed by students as ancient and boring, without any relevance for their lives. Making Shakespeare come alive for students is a perennial challenge. In this vignette, a teacher of gifted adolescents uses assessment as a mechanism to draw the students into *Othello* while also challenging their analytic skills and using the assessment to gauge both individual and collective skills of comprehension and analysis of characters during the reading of the play. The task is described in Table 7.1, the assignment handout for the students.

This task was explicitly designed to engage the students in thoughtful attention to various characters, with some personal investment in getting to know them well. The teacher preselected characters and scenes to ensure that all characters were discussed as they developed throughout the play. On a more practical note, he was also able to schedule the students' presentations and individual preconferences. The assignment was not a trivial undertaking and required considerable advance instruction and practice so that the students were ready to tackle it. They had already studied plays and how they are structured, the sociopolitical structures and cultural values of the Elizabethan and Jacobean periods, and how literary terminology and literary devices work to create vivid images and lead the audience. The teacher had also provided many organizers for making oral presentations and supporting their comments.

Although the complete *Othello* unit addressed more than character revelation, this assessment process, designed to motivate and promote learning, gave the teacher access to the thinking and understanding of his students individually and collectively. The conferences, coupled with the teacher's ongoing observation and questioning in class, offered tremendous scope for altering the pace, reviewing or reteaching concepts, solving problems collectively, or doing whatever seemed appropriate given the group's perception of need.

The rubric that the teacher and students used following the initial conference is included in Table 7.2. Although rubrics come up later in Chapter 9, please note that this one has detailed descriptors of the "look fors" in this assignment as a foundation for discussion and clarification. There is no suggestion that the teacher intends to use the rubric for marking or grading the assignment. It is a tool for discussion and an aid for the student to refine the presentation for the "public" exhibition in front of the class.

In an ongoing conversation with this teacher, we have started to explore the adjectives that differentiate his Levels, with the intent of making these targets more concrete for the students.

Table 7.1 Student Handout for *Othello* Character Revelation Assignment

Individual Character Revelation in Othello

Character Revelation

Throughout the play, various characters win your sympathy, stir your ire, excite your frustration, or inspire your contentment. Indeed, many characters have the power to evoke a myriad of responses from the audience throughout the production. The capacity for this lies in the playwright's ability to create characters that may grow from static creations to emotionally and intellectually charged human beings whose desires, motives, and actions can be readily understood and believed by the audience. Authentic characters must evolve within the context of conflicts, relationships, emerging action, and plot development. Each of these elements provides an avenue through which the playwright reveals the true nature of the character, and the audience comes to understand, contemplate, and even judge the merits of characters within the context of the play.

Each student has been assigned one character from a particular scene in the play.

The Task

You must each do a character analysis, with particular attention to your respective scene, to determine how the character has developed or is further revealed to the audience. You will apply prior context of the character's revelation up to that scene, but the focus of the inquiry and analysis should remain within the scene itself. More specifically, the focus within the scene should be directed toward three areas that help reveal characters: dramatic function, relationships, and language.

- *Dramatic Function.* In this area of inquiry, you are interested in how a character's role is used to move the action or conflict forward or aid in the development of the plot. You need to ask questions about the character's role and determine how the role is manifested in the scene. Some possible questions are, What is your character's relationship to the central events in the play? How does the character function to support central events, themes, or conflicts? What is your character's relationship to other characters in the play? Might he or she act as a foil to another character? How does the nature of your character shape or motivate the necessary actions and responses that such a role demands?
- *Relationships.* This area of inquiry requires a consideration of the character through observation of behavior and attitudes borne out of human relationships. Characters are often best understood relative to others. This allows the audience to make value judgments regarding a character's interaction with others in various situations.

(Continued)

Table 7.1 (*Continued*)

Individual Character Revelation in Othello

Some possible questions are, How would you define the prevailing attitude of your character? What underlying emotions motivate the actions of your character? What attitudes or perspectives are displayed in your scene? Are these consistent with your previous understanding of his or her nature? How has your character changed from the opening scene, and do you foresee more changes? What other characters seem to affect your character most? Why?

- *Language.* The power that a playwright uses to create authentic characters and moments on stage exists in the ability to manipulate language. The poetry of Shakespeare (remember, Shakespeare called himself a "poet," not a "playwright") helps to reveal his characters, especially considering the array of literary devices that he employs. He uses metaphors and similes. He uses rhyme. He uses tone and diction as well. Some questions to consider: What literary devices does Shakespeare use to expose your character's nature? How does the choice of diction relate to your character's status, attitude, education, passion, intelligence, humor, and so on? Does this change at all? If so, why? How might the character's tone be understood as a reflection of his or her nature? Why?

Ultimately, you will present your ideas orally to the rest of the class when we, as a group, reach that particular scene during our in-class reading. One week before the class presentation, you will meet with me in a conference and deliver your character revelations. The conference should last about 15 minutes, and you should be prepared to offer between 5 and 10 minutes of material for us to discuss. After the conference, both you and I will use the attached rubric to assess the character revelation. We will meet the subsequent day to discuss our perspectives, and you can use this feedback to prepare for the class presentation.

Assessment to Reverse Socialization

Teachers need to keep in mind another motivational issue. External assessments and routine reporting requirements can have a demotivating effect on students. Students enter school already socialized by the long-standing history of schools as places where they are judged and marked, often with important consequences (from parental reactions, to entry to further and higher education). These factors tend to focus pupil attention on meeting demands rather than on any intangible personal benefits of the learning. For some, the certainty of praise and success in this enterprise has become a drug; they continually

(Text continues on page 76)

Table 7.2 Character Revelation Rubric

Level	Dramatic Function	Character's Relationships	Character's Language
5	• Character's response to events, conflict, or action within the scene clearly identified, *insightfully*, thoroughly, and *confidently* explained using *superior* range and depth of relevant textual support • Motives for character's behavior within the scene clearly identified, *insightfully*, thoroughly, and *confidently* explained using superior range and depth of relevant textual support • Character's contribution to conflict and/or plot development clearly identified, *insightfully*, thoroughly, and *confidently* explained using *superior* range and depth of relevant textual support	• Character's attitudes toward other characters clearly identified, *insightfully*, thoroughly, and *confidently* explained using *superior* range and depth of relevant textual support • Character's historic and developing relationships clearly identified, *insightfully*, thoroughly, and *confidently* explained using *superior* range and depth of relevant textual support • Demonstrates a thorough and *insightful* understanding of motives behind character's actions, and responses to other characters, using *superior* range and depth of relevant textual support	• Clearly identifies, *insightfully*, thoroughly, and *confidently* explains how a character's diction reveals his or her status and perspective, using three *effective* examples from the text • Clearly identifies, *insightfully*, thoroughly, and *confidently* explains how literary devices serve to reflect the character's attitude or point of view, using three *effective* examples from the text • Clearly identifies, *insightfully*, thoroughly, and *confidently* explains the consistency or shift in character's tone that reveals the character's stage(s) of development, *effectively* using language from the beginning, middle, and end of the scene
4	• Character's response to events, conflict, or action within the scene *clearly* identified and	• Character's attitude toward other characters *clearly* identified and *thoroughly* explained	• Clearly identifies and *thoroughly* explains how a character's diction reveals his or her status and

(Continued)

Table 7.2 *(Continued)*

Level	Dramatic Function	Character's Relationships	Character's Language
	thoroughly explained using *relevant* textual support • Motives for character's behavior within the scene *clearly* identified and *thoroughly* explained using *relevant* textual support • Character's contribution to conflict and/or plot development *clearly* identified and *thoroughly* explained using *relevant* textual support	using *relevant* textual support • Character's historic and developing relationships *clearly* identified and *thoroughly* explained using *relevant* textual support • Demonstrates a *thorough* understanding of motives behind character's actions, and responses to other characters, using *relevant* textual support	perspective, using *three relevant* examples from the text • Clearly identifies, *thoroughly* explains how literary devices serve to reflect the character's attitude or point of view, using *three* relevant examples from the text • Clearly identifies and *thoroughly* explains the consistency or shift in character's tone that reveals the character's stage(s) of development, using *relevant* language from the beginning, middle, and end of the scene
3	• Character's response to events, conflict, or action within the scene *identified* and *explained* with *some* reference to characters or events in the text • Motives for character's behavior within the scene *identified* and *explained* with *some* reference to characters or events in the text	• Character's attitude toward other characters *identified* and explained using some textual support • Character's historic and developing relationships with other characters *identified* and *explained* with *some* reference to characters and events in the text • Demonstrates an *adequate*	• *Identifies* and *explains* how a character's diction reveals his or her status and perspective, using at *least two* examples from the text • *Identifies* and *explains* how literary devices serve to reflect the character's attitude or point of view, using at *least two* examples from the text

(Continued)

Table 7.2 *(Continued)*

Level	Dramatic Function	Character's Relationships	Character's Language
	• Character's contribution to conflict and/or plot development *identified* and *explained* with *some* reference to characters and events in the text	understanding of motives behind character's actions, and responses to other characters, using *some* reference to characters and events in the text	• *Identifies* and *explains* the consistency or shift in character's tone that reveals the character's stage(s) of development, using language from two *different parts* of the scene
2	• Character's response to events, conflict, or action within the scene only *partly identified or explained* • Motives for character's behavior within the scene *only partly identified or explained* • Character's contribution to conflict and/or plot development only *partly identified or explained*	• *Partially* demonstrates the character's attitude toward other characters in the text • Character's historic or developing relationships with other characters only *partly identified or explained* • Demonstrates *partial* understanding of motives behind character's actions and/or responses to other characters	• *Partially* identifies or explains how a character's diction reveals his or her status and perspective, with *some* reference to language in the text • *Partially* identifies or explains how literary devices serve to reflect the character's attitude or point of view, with *some* reference to language in the text • *Partially* identifies or explains the consistency or shift in character's tone that reveals the character's stage(s) of development, with *some* reference to language in the text

(Continued)

Table 7.2 *(Continued)*

Level	Dramatic Function	Character's Relationships	Character's Language
1	• Character's response to events, conflict, or action within the *scene not identified or unable to be explained* • Motives for character's behavior within the scene *not identified or unable to be explained* • Character's contribution to conflict and/or plot development *not identified or unable to be explained*	• *Cannot* coherently demonstrate the character's attitude toward other characters in the text • Character's historic or developing relationships with other *characters not identified or unable to be explained* • Demonstrates *little to no* understanding of motives behind character's actions or responses to other characters	• *Cannot* identify or explain how a character's diction reveals his or her status and perspective • *Cannot* identify or explain how literary devices serve to reflect the character's attitude or point of view • *Cannot* identify or explain the consistency or shift in character's tone that reveals the character's stage(s) of development

need more. For many other students, year upon year of "not good enough" has eroded their intellectual self-confidence and resulted in a kind of mind-numbing malaise.

Teachers can use assessment to foster motivation to learn, not just to pass the test. But breaking old habits will not be easy. Instead, it will be a long process of little steps, with setbacks and failures along the way. Nevertheless, I believe it is worth taking up the challenge. When assessment is integrated into the learning process, students and teachers can work together with a shared expectation of finding out what makes sense. This can unleash students' natural curiosity and encourage them to engage in the work in order to acquire knowledge or skills. I have to repeat, however, that the process will take time. Changes this dramatic cannot be accomplished abruptly. Any meaningful reordering of important phases of instruction takes time, but teachers, students, and parents can develop the dispositions and habits of mind of taking learning seriously, recognizing the value or assessment for learning, and seeing assessment as a positive experience. Like all socializing activities, these kinds of dispositions develop gradually, in this case, through exposure to a different kind of assessment experience.

Traditional Assessment *of* Learning is not likely to disappear, nor should it. The trick is to balance its effects by ensuring that students have alternative views about themselves and their learning, and that these views are valued and shared as well. Over the long run, the cumulative effect of Assessment *for* Learning and Assessment *as* Learning should encourage students to develop motivation to learn as an enduring disposition.

Ideas for Follow-Up

1. Examine a sample of your assessment strategies. How relevant are they? How much do they capture the imagination? What information do they provide to the student that can scaffold learning?

2. How might these assessment strategies be modified to make them better motivators for student learning?

3. What changes might you make in your classroom assessment as a result of your discussions about using assessment as motivation?

CHAPTER

Using Assessment to Make Connections

In Chapter 4, I talked about how learning is different for novices and experts and the stages in between. Biggs and Collis (1982) studied students as they responded to questions in a variety of subjects in classrooms. They characterized the responses of the students in five categories:

- *Prestructural level.* The student had little idea about how to approach a new idea, so he or she produced an irrelevant response or no response to questions posed.

- *Unistructural level.* The student selected one piece of information and focused on it, with no attention to other details.

- *Multistructural level.* The student focused on more than one piece of information but made no attempt to link one piece to another.

- *Relational level.* The student tied several pieces of information together under headings or categories.

- *Extended abstract level.* The student took the categorized information and carried it into new areas or ideas.

This conception of learning draws attention to the value of depth of learning, rather than coverage. It highlights that teaching is enabling others to learn by finding ways of helping each student see the connections among the bits of information and relate new ideas to his or her previous understanding. The focus shifts from presenting the same information to all students at the same time to helping individual students see their own learning in relation to personal markers, as well as to external ones. For many people, learning feels like a random activity. It just seems to happen (or it doesn't). Unless a person knows how to order his or her thoughts, attention goes to whatever is in the immediate environment, and the learner will often wallow in confusion and uncertainty, without any mechanisms for bringing order to things. But learning can be controlled and enhanced by focusing attempts to make sense of information in order to relate it to prior knowledge and master the skills involved.

In the early stages of learning something new, students (regardless of their age) need supporting structures and rules to give them a framework for seeing patterns. As their learning becomes more complex and they internalize these organizers, they are able to work with and sometimes even construct new ones that reflect combinations of, sophisticated connections to, and subtle changes to the originals. These organizers allow students to monitor what is being learned and use the feedback from this monitoring to make adjustments, adaptations, and even major changes in what is understood. These organizers also help students come to understand that learning is not a random accumulation of bits of information. Rather, it is a dynamic process of making sense of ideas by manipulating, altering, and transforming them in their heads. The most important learning becomes the students' own learning and its progress over time. Unfortunately, many see little connection between the bits of information that accrue at school and the world that they experience after school lets out for the day. Teachers are the only bridge that can connect them. These connections are much more likely when students can see what they are aiming for, have organizational structures to help them see the connections, and can make personal connections between their expectations and their own view of the world.

> People learn best when they make connections between what they already know and what they are learning, when they can draw on their experiences and make greater meaning of them, when they see how ideas relate to one another, and when they can use what they are learning in concrete ways.
>
> —Darling-Hammond (1992)

Curricula as Visible Targets for Learning

As Black and Wiliam (1998) found, learning is easier when both the teacher and the student have a clear image of where they are headed. This is not to say that they need a long list of the bits of information that they need to store inside their brains. Rather, teachers need a big picture of the whole course or learning agenda to frame the learning tasks. They also need more detailed breakdowns that identify the inter-relationships and connections embedded in the concepts, skills, and knowledge that make up the successful learning so that they can create appropriate activities along the way.

> Students can reach any targets that they can see and that stand still for them.
>
> —Stiggins (1993)

Students also need to see the big picture to make it worth their while to travel this road. All too often, we ask students to get on the "learning train" with no idea of what the desti-nation will be or why they should go there. When they know the purpose and direction of their learning and can see the connection of the learn-ing intention of any particular task to the larger agenda, they are likely to be more motivated and task-oriented. Even more important, they can plan their own learning and see their own progress.

Mapping the relationships may seem straightforward, but this process is much more than a scope-and-sequence chart. The goal is to make the next step in learning visible to the students so that they can use their minds to unravel ideas and see patterns.

As I mentioned in Chapter 2, content standards are a legacy of large-scale reform. These standards provide a starting point for teachers to articulate the learning targets for their classes. Fortunately, the standards that have been developed, especially by subject organizations, include challenging subject matter and describe what it means to know and learn in each of these disciplines. I have included a segment from the National Council of Teachers of Mathematics (NCTM) standards in Table 8.1 as an example to show the richness and detail that the stan-dards can provide.

> Learning is seeing patterns in the world around us. Teaching is creating the conditions in which students can see the known patterns of our collective understanding. Nobel prize winners see patterns where they have not been seen before.
>
> —John Polanyi, Nobel Laureate–Chemistry

As you can see, these standards offer a worthy starting place for cre-ating the day-to-day work of teachers and students. They can serve many purposes, from stimulating the beginning of a conversation about what should be taught in schools and at what level; to guiding the program planning for teachers; to describ-ing detailed benchmarks, with examples of what is expected of students.

Table 8.1   NCTM Measurement Standard: "Applying Appropriate Techniques, Tools, and Formulas to Determine Measurements"

Grade	Standard
Pre-K-2	• Measure with multiple copies of units of the same size, such as paper clips laid end to end • Use repetition of a single unit to measure something larger than the unit, for instance, measuring the length of a room with a single meter stick • Use tools to measure • Develop common referents for measures to make comparisons and estimates
3–5	• Develop strategies for estimating the perimeters, areas, and volumes of irregular shapes • Select and apply appropriate standard units and tools to measure length, area, volume, weight, time, temperature, and the size of angles • Select and use benchmarks to estimate measurements • Develop, understand, and use formulas to find the area of rectangles and related triangles and parallelograms • Develop strategies to determine the surface areas and volumes of rectangular solids
6–8	• Use common benchmarks to select appropriate methods for estimating measurements • Select and apply techniques and tools to accurately find length, area, volume, and angle measures to appropriate levels of precision • Develop and use formulas to determine the circumference of circles and the area of triangles, parallelograms, trapezoids, and circles, and develop strategies to find the area of more complex shapes • Develop strategies to determine the surface area and volume of selected prisms, pyramids, and cylinders • Solve problems involving scale factors, using ratio and proportion • Solve simple problems involving rates and derived measurements for such attributes as velocity and density
9–12	• Analyze precision, accuracy, and approximate error in measurement situations • Understand and use formulas for the area, surface area, and volume of geometric figures, including cones, spheres, and cylinders • Apply informal concepts of successive approximation, upper and lower bounds, and limit in measurement situations • Use unit analysis to check measurement computations

SOURCE: Reprinted with permission from *Principles and Standards for School Mathematics*, copyright 2000 by the National Council of Teachers of Mathematics. All rights reserved.

The power comes not from having standards or objectives, but from routinely using them to clarify what the learning is about and how it all connects. Curriculum expectations have always been used to judge students' performance, or as reference points for a process of deriving information from students in order to modify teaching. If assessment is going to link curriculum to student learning, then standards must become the "stuff" of discussion in classes. All too often, students have very little understanding of the purpose of classroom activities or of the assessment tasks. If they are going to take responsibility for their own learning, they need to know what the "grand scheme" is and how the piece with which they are working fits. A simple chart of curriculum objectives on the classroom wall can be useful for students as they are working; so can regular statements of the intent of the learning throughout a lesson or a unit. Students also need to be able to distinguish between what teachers want them to do, what they want them to learn, how teachers and the students themselves will know what they have achieved, and what comes next.

Although curriculum standards provide an image of what students are expected to learn, they do not give a sense of how the students should go about the learning process. Often, students are expected to think about something without having learned how to think or having practiced thinking. Thinking, however, is a multifaceted, complex neural activity that requires a range of prior skill development. Art Costa and Bena Kallick (2000) have produced a series of books focused on what they call "habits of mind." The basic premise is that young people (and adults, for that matter) can come to deeper understanding and do much better on critical and creative thinking tasks when they are taught and internalize these habits of mind. Simply, habits of mind are "broad, enduring and essential life-span learnings" (p. xiii). These include persistence; listening with understanding and empathy; questioning and posing problems; applying past knowledge to new situations;

> Habits give control over the environment, power to utilize it for human purposes. Active habits involve thought, invention, and initiative in applying capacities to new aims. They are opposed to routine, which marks an arrest of growth. Since growth is the characteristic of life, education is all one with growing; it has no end beyond itself. The criterion of the value of school education is the extent in which it creates a desire for continued growth.
>
> —Dewey (1916)

gathering data through all of the senses; and creating, imagining, and innovating. Habits of mind obviously do not replace standard curriculum or teaching. They complement and extend it by explicitly pushing the limits on students' thinking and equipping them with tools to go the distance in both school and life. Orchestrating the conditions for students to make connections and use their developing habits of mind requires careful planning on the part of teachers, individually and together.

Plan Learning, Plan Assessment, and Expect the Unexpected

Learning is not a linear process. Assessment doesn't come at the end. Teaching is not the filling in the sandwich between curriculum and assessment. Taken together, curriculum, teaching, learning, and assessment interact in an iterative and sometimes cyclical process. They feed into one another and sometimes dart back and forth in seemingly unpredictable patterns. This does not mean that they are independent of or disconnected from one another. On the contrary, the interconnections are key. Curriculum, teaching, and assessment all need to be consistent for effective learning. If teachers are going to see the connections and recognize trends, they will need to map the curriculum topic by topic and identify the threads of skills and learning that make up the program—horizontally, to see what is intended for this class, and vertically, to follow the progressions that will occur across classes, subjects, and years (Sutton, 1995). All of this means that the curriculum is not the first element of planning that teachers should consider. Learning intentions and assessment are connected so closely to curriculum that it is impossible to plan them in isolation from one another.

This is not to suggest that planning should set the day in stone. The wonderful thing about planning is that once you've done it, you can make all kinds of changes and adjustments and not lose the plot. Or, if you do, it's on purpose. Careful planning is the skeleton for the school day. You can't see it, but its absence would be a disaster. Plans should provide the blueprint and the organizers that teachers and students can use to constantly identify the intentions, make the connections explicit, reinforce the relationships, and identify the misconceptions that can get in the way. Whether or not activities are appropriate and fulfill learning intentions should be in constant question. Ongoing assessment is the key to making on-the-spot corrections or modifications, or even abandoning the whole thing for another direction.

"The Case of the Literacy Hour"

During the past 4 years, I have been involved in the external evaluation of the National Literacy and Numeracy Strategies in England (Earl et al., 2000). One of the characteristics of the literacy strategy is the organization of material and the focus on teaching within a Literacy Hour, with clear curriculum targets. At the same time, there are high-profile national numerical targets for schools. The Secretary of State for Education has publicly stated that he would resign his post if the targets of 80% achieving level 4 in literacy and 75% reaching level 4 in mathematics by 2002 were not reached. Each school has set annual percentage targets that are reported and monitored regularly to see how it is doing. A public and numeric process like this runs the risk of focusing attention on students as "widgets." "If I can just get Sonia over the bar, we'll be OK." The Directorate of the Strategies, however, has put considerable effort into making the connections between the National Curriculum and target setting for schools. Teachers are encouraged to think about curriculum targets and what they mean for individual students.

I have been lucky enough to observe some talented teachers who have internalized and are using the target-setting exercise as more than a quantitative series of ticks on a record sheet. They are using the curriculum targets to clarify the learning goals and establish the criteria of quality for individual tasks. From then on, modifying them for individual children or groups of children is relatively straightforward.

In a small, rural primary school, the Year 3 (Grade 2) teacher started the lesson with a whole-group activity—shared reading of a Big Book. This book, about a youngster and his experience with growing vegetables that took over the garden, had been introduced to the class the day before, so they spent a few minutes reviewing the title, the author, the picture on the cover, and what they had read the day before, and they made predictions about what might happen next in the story. Then, several of the children each read a portion of the book aloud, as did the teacher. During the shared reading, the teacher routinely drew attention to how the author used descriptive words to help the reader see the images in the story, even without looking at the pictures. On the blackboard behind her head was the curriculum target for the day: *Objective: Identify and use expressive, figurative, and descriptive language, especially adjectives, to create effects in poetry and prose.*

A class lesson followed in which the teacher read the objective aloud to the children and discussed what it meant, reviewing with them the terms *adjective, expressive, figurative,* and *descriptive.* She then explained to the class that adjectives could be used to create interesting effects in writing—to cause a feeling or an emotion in the reader or to try to make an image or a picture of the object in the mind of the reader. During this part of the lesson, she showed the children some simple sentences she had already written on the board and asked them to try to think of interesting adjectives to help a reader get a feeling or create a mental picture about the object in the sentence. Children enthusiastically raised their hands to offer suggestions. The teacher took a half-dozen suggestions in turn, each discussed by teacher and child with a combination of questioning—"Why did you choose the word *massive?*" "And does that adjective, *massive,* tell us something about the zucchini?" "Think carefully. Is that word, *massive,* an adjective?"—and careful explanations of what made a good response. Several examples were worked in this way. The children seemed eager to offer suggestions and attempt explanations, and the teacher praised the efforts of all who volunteered—"Excellent," or "That was a great try, but *nice* doesn't really describe the zucchini. We want a word to describe the zucchini that would help the reader see what the author had in mind. How would *nice* do that?"

When a child gave an evocative response, she modeled writing for the children by writing the new sentence on the board as the child repeated it. At one point, she misspelled a word deliberately to be greeted by a show of hands eager to help her out. She found this was something that gave the children great delight and helped to keep some of them focused during this part of the lesson.

After this sentence-level teaching session was finished, the teacher told the class that the group activities for today would continue working with figurative language by using adjectives, or *words that describe an object or tell you something about the object that makes it easier for the reader to picture it.* She was going to work with one group to construct sentences about plants using adjectives. The other groups were each going to their tables to work on the assignments she had placed there for them. Propped on each table was the specific target for the day: *using expressive, figurative, and descriptive language, especially adjectives, to create effects in prose.*

When the teacher was working in the guided writing exercise with the small group, she was observing, asking questions, and making on-the-spot adjustments to fill in the gaps in each child's learning. I listened for a while as she worked with them. Instruction and assessment were seamless. She was regularly reiterating the goals ("We're using descriptive adjectives to help readers make a picture in their mind, to make others see the plants the way we want them to be seen"); providing examples ("How about a nubbly pumpkin?"); and asking focused questions ("What did the sunflower look like? How did it feel?"). The children were having a ball thinking of words to make ordinary plants into exciting images, such as "wispy dandelions" and "terrified tomatoes," and explaining why the adjectives that they were suggesting were exactly the right ones for the impression that they were trying to make. All the while, the teacher was listening and probing to get a sense of their understanding and using her analysis to focus and extend their learning.

The rest of the class was equally busy. In one group, the students were completing a "cloze" passage that required them to insert reasonable adjectives from a list the teacher had set out on a laminated sheet. In another, the task was more open-ended. The students were writing short sentences using adjectives and nouns from lists set out for them. A fourth group was revising a short passage by crossing out the existing adjectives and replacing them with more expressive or imaginative adjectives. Afterwards, she explained that the tasks had been created for different groups based on her assessment of the practice that would help them now.

Although the teacher was completely occupied with one group, the rest of the students were producing paper artifacts that she could quickly scan and also read more carefully later. She spent a few minutes with each group asking pointed questions and checking the level of understanding. In the next phase of the Literacy Hour, she moved into a brief plenary session in which she pulled together the ideas and used the children's work from all of the groups to illustrate the power of adjectives. As a finale, the children identified the image that they found the most interesting, and some of them described it to the class in words and explained why they thought it was interesting. You might say that this example sounds more like instruction than assessment. And you would be partially right. The teacher began with key objectives that were readily visible and gave the children a clear sense of the learning expectations. The assessment happened throughout the lesson and the group work in ways that contributed to learning. The intimate connection between instruction and assessment was evident in the questions that the teacher asked and in the students whom she chose to answer them. It showed in the choices of assignments for the groups' independent work, and it guided the decisions that the teacher made about how to conduct the plenary session. This is "scaffolding" in action: students and the teacher engaged in challenging conversation and questioning to elicit and embed understanding.

Differentiation

Differentiation is making sure that the right students get the right learning tasks at the right time. Once you have a sense of what each student holds as "given" or "known" and what he or she needs in order to learn, differentiation is no longer an option. It is an obvious response. But it can be a formidable task. To many of you, it probably feels like a recipe for failure. How can you possibly individualize teaching for all of those students, especially in secondary schools, where you see more than 100 students a day?

Differentiation doesn't mean a different program for each student in the class, and it doesn't mean ability grouping to reduce the differences. It means recognizing and accepting that each student is a unique individual. It means using what you know about learning and about each student to improve your teaching so that students all work in ways that have an optimal effect on their learning. And assessment provides the necessary information to do it.

Ruth Sutton (1995) says it best:

> The key to effective differentiation is the accuracy and relevance of the information that we use to decide appropriate learning tasks for pupils, and our willingness to challenge these decisions from time to time by allowing students to surprise us. (p. 26)

All too often, we confuse children's lack of experience with lack of ability. We view diversity as limiting and slow down instruction rather than accelerating it. Instead of delaying learning, we should be finding a different approach to learning to meet the special needs and unique qualities of each student. Assessment, instead of being the means for categorizing students and avoiding working to help them learn, becomes the mechanism for deciding what to do to push the learning forward.

When teachers are asked about the factors that affect learning, they mention things like those listed in Table 8.2. Most of these will be familiar. They are qualities that differentiate all students, not just a few of them labeled as "special needs."

Finding out about students as learners and as people is the key to differentiation. When teachers are equipped with detailed knowledge about their students and have a clear idea about what the students need to learn, differentiation can happen all of the time. If the lesson is in science, but reading the instructions is hampering some students, the teacher can read the instructions for some of them or write instructions that are succinct and short so that those who are daunted by a lot of reading feel comfortable. If the mathematics task in the next unit requires that the students have a solid grasp of basic shapes, the teacher can use manipulatives, at the beginning of the class for a few days before, to review the material, ascertain the nature of each student's understanding, and provide support. Activities like the Pool Table task provide every student with access to the ideas and give

Table 8.2   Factors That Affect Students' Learning

- Reading ability, confidence, and speed
- Writing ability, confidence, and speed
- Concentration span
- Spatial awareness
- Hand-eye coordination
- Ability to listen to instructions and absorb information aurally
- Ability to absorb information visually, from pictures or diagrams
- Skill in manipulating numbers
- Functioning of the senses, particularly sight and hearing
- Learning styles (i.e., the approach to learning with which the learner feels most comfortable, and the ability to learn in different ways when the circumstances change)
- Previous experience, knowledge, and skills
- Support and encouragement from parents
- Self-esteem
- High or low expectations from themselves, peers, their families, and their teachers
- The belief among teachers and schools that they can make a difference

SOURCE: Sutton (1995).

teachers a chance to work with some students as they do it. Individual attention can be focused on what they need to do now to move on in their learning. What insights can teachers help them achieve? What is the next obvious piece in this puzzle?

Ideas for Follow-Up

1.   Pick a student in your class. Make a detailed list of what you know about this student's learning, about the conditions in which the student learns best, about the patterns with which he or she is familiar, about his or her learning habits and prior knowledge and learning style, and so on.

2.   Now think about a unit you are currently teaching. What patterns are you trying to make visible for students? What are the learning targets? What are the essential qualities of successful mastery?

3.   How can you match what you know about the student with the curricular expectations?

Using Assessment to Extend Learning

By now it should be obvious that assessment is an integral part of learning. It provides a window into how and what students are thinking and signals the kind of feedback that is necessary to support learning. As I discussed in Chapter 6, diagnostic assessment provides feedback to teachers about student learning so that they can use it to coordinate teaching and tailor support for students. From the research that has been done so far, assessment is such a valuable part of learning because it can make learning visible to both teachers and students.

Feedback for Learning

It isn't enough for teachers to see the next steps and use them in their planning. Students need to see them as well. Feedback for learning is the process that provides the conceptual link between what students believe to be true and the collective wisdom of the culture as it is captured in the knowledge carried by teachers and in the texts, resources, and so on that are available to them as reference points. As Grant Wiggins (1993) puts it, "Feedback is information that provides the performer with direct, useable insights into current performance, based on tangible differences between current performance and hoped for performance" (p. 182).

Feedback can lead to increased effort or engagement, alternative strategies to understand the material, and the restructuring of understanding. A major role for teachers in the learning process is to provide the kind of feedback to students that encourages their learning and provides signposts and directions along the way, bringing them closer to independence.

Feedback for learning can take many forms. It can be formal or informal. It can be individual or collective. Feedback can also be evaluative or descriptive, as Caroline Gipps and her colleagues (Gipps et al., 2000) have described it (see Table 9.1).

> Feedback can be the vital link between the teachers' assessment of a child and the action following that assessment, which then has a formative effect on the child's learning.
>
> —Hargreaves et al. (2000)

All too often, teachers provide evaluative feedback in the form of grades and short (usually nonspecific) comments, often praise or censure. This kind of feedback tells students whether they are okay or not and affects their sense of themselves and their position in relation to learning, but it offers little direction for moving their learning forward. Thinking back to the earlier comments about motivation, evaluative feedback leaves students feeling either good or bad about themselves, without any sense of what is inspiring their feeling except the external symbol of their success or lack of it. Some of them have a momentary feeling of self-esteem, especially in relation to a social comparison with their peers. Others are left to lick their wounds. After a while, learning, and even school itself, is pushed into a less important role in their lives, as they use the negative feedback to discount school and adjust their expectations in other directions.

Descriptive feedback, on the other hand, makes explicit connections between students' thinking and other possibilities that they should consider. It is linked to the learning that is expected. It addresses faulty interpretations and lack of understanding. It provides students with visible and manageable "next steps" based on an assessment of the work at hand and an image of what "good work looks like" so that they can begin to take on the responsibility of self-assessing and self-correcting. Feedback is not an independent activity. Rather, it is part of the teaching process—the part that comes after the initial instruction takes place, when information is provided based on the way that the individual has processed and interpreted the original material.

When students are aware of the reason for the task, see the task as possible, and know what they are striving for, they are almost always motivated to go for it. Good feedback keeps this activity in balance. It allows them to set reasonable goals, track their performance, and set the next goal in the ongoing process of learning.

In a wonderful book called *Unlocking Formative Assessment*, Shirley Clarke (2001), from the Institute for Education at the University of London, describes her program of research directed at understanding

Table 9.1   Evaluative and Descriptive Feedback Strategies

Evaluative feedback	• Giving rewards and punishments • Expressing approval and disapproval
Descriptive feedback	• Telling children they are right or wrong • Describing why an answer is correct • Telling children what they have achieved and have not achieved • Specifying or implying a better way of doing something • Getting children to suggest ways they can improve

SOURCE: Gipps et al. (2000).

feedback and how it works. Although she is working in primary classes and concentrating on literacy, the principles that she describes hold the promise of being generalizable to many settings and age groups. In her research, she has found that feedback is most useful when it focuses on the learning intentions of the task. She advocates displaying the specific learning intentions for the lesson or unit prominently in the classroom and regularly returning to them throughout the lesson, as the central focus of the work. While the students are working on a task, it is easy for the teacher to be distracted by other occurrences or behaviors. The message to the students, however, is that student behavior, being neat, and so on are more important than the lesson at hand, and they get distracted as well. Instead, the teacher's major focus should be feedback to individuals and groups that helps them to see the ideas and make the connections in their thinking.

Clarke (2001) also tackles the sticky issue of how to give feedback on written work to guide students' learning. She suggests focusing feedback on a few things that are directly connected to the learning intentions for the task. She uses simple strategies, such as using a highlighter pen to identify examples of the learning intentions in the child's work, selecting a few of these highlighted elements to show where some improvement could be made, drawing an arrow from the selected items to a white space on the page, and writing what she calls a "closing the gap" prompt—prompts for making changes to their work that are geared to the particular student and what the teacher already knows about that student. Table 9.2 is an example from her book.

It is interesting to me that teachers often use reminder prompts when students would benefit from more structure and could be pushed in their learning with scaffolding prompts. Often, when students see example prompts, they immediately produce their own

Table 9.2   An Example of Possible Closing-the-Gap Prompts

Learning Intention: To effectively introduce a character at the start of a story.

Activity: Choose someone you know but the class doesn't to describe in a written paragraph.

We are Learning to: Write about people's characters for our stories.

How Will We Know We've Done It? (created with the class): We will have written something about their appearance, their likes and dislikes, their personality, their attitudes, and other things that help others know more about them.

Let's assume that a child has written about someone he knows from a summer camp. After highlighting several phrases that successfully give information about this person, the teacher asterisks the phrase "This person is a good friend." The arrow to the closing-the-gap prompt could take any of the following forms:

A Reminder Prompt: Say more about how you feel about this person.
  A reminder prompt is most suitable for a student who probably has a good command of figurative language but has not used it here, for whatever reason.

A Scaffolding Prompt: Can you describe how this person is a good friend? (question) Or, Describe something that happened that showed you what a good friend this person is. (directive) Or, He showed me he was a good friend when . . . (finish the sentence).
Scaffolding prompts work well with students who need more structure or some direction but are likely to carry on from here.

An Example Prompt: Choose one of these sentences to tell me more about your friend. "He is a good friend because he never says unkind things about me." Or, "My friend helps me do things."
When students are struggling or don't appear to understand the concept, example prompts can provide them with actual models of the learning intention.

SOURCE: Adapted from Clarke (2001).

improvement and go beyond the teacher's expectations. Students are very motivated by these closing-the-gap strategies, and teachers are astounded by how quickly and thoughtfully they respond. A number of exciting spin-offs have come from this approach to feedback in marking. Once students get the hang of it, it lends itself to self- and paired student marking. Students start to think about what the teacher would highlight, develop arguments and reasons for their choices, offer one another suggestions for improvement, and revisit their own work with a critical eye.

As with all feedback, the quality of students' work depends on the quality of the closing-the-gap comments. Just giving feedback is not necessarily useful and may not even be motivating. By itself, feedback has no power to initiate action. Instead, it is a signpost or a guide for consideration by the student, which is all the more reason for providing the kind of high-quality feedback that makes the links between the current state of knowledge and the target. When feedback is vague or faulty, students make inappropriate modifications or don't see any reason to learn more or make adjustments to their thinking.

Although teachers are the most obvious purveyors of feedback, they are not the only ones. Peers and parents are just as important. Why? Because learning is social. Early experiential knowledge forms the fabric of children's lives and is often resistant to change. It is the "stuff" that life has taught them. People are constantly testing the veracity of their beliefs and ideas (and those of their community and culture) by comparing them to the beliefs and ideas held by the people around them. This testing process often involves books, media, and other resources, but the key contributors to the internal dialogue for students are teachers, parents, and peers.

So, what does good feedback look like? Good feedback provides evidence that confirms or refutes an idea. It gives students a chance to reflect on their learning and their learning needs. It gives recognition and appropriate praise for achievement and growth. It is targeted to the specific learning needs of each student or group of students. It gives clear directions for improvement and allows students the time to think about and respond to the suggestions. Finally, it focuses on quality and learning.

Although it is difficult to describe the iterative nature of feedback, I think it is important to reinforce that it is an ongoing process. When the process of feedback is running smoothly, it is a reciprocal flow of influence (Senge, 1990). Teachers use assessment to provide feedback to students about their conceptions and misconceptions; students use their feedback from teachers to adjust their understandings, rethink their ideas, and put their new conceptions forward, leading to another round of feedback and another extension of the learning. This process doesn't happen after the fact, or even once a term. It is part of a continuous conversation between teachers and students and among students.

When feedback is descriptive and iterative, it has a very different effect on the students' perceptions of themselves as learners and their overall self-esteem. When students see the effects of their efforts and know what comes next, they are more likely to remain motivated and to see how their progress is linked to their work.

Rubrics and Exemplars as Tools

I laughed recently when a teacher in a professional development session asked me if I was there to "rubricize" him. It sounded like an inoculation was all that he needed to gain access to this magical world of rubrics. There is no doubt that rubrics have become the "flavor of the year" in education; you have already seen several rubrics in earlier chapters. In this chapter, I expand on the use of rubrics and give some suggestions about how to make them effective. Unfortunately, many people still cling to the notion that the purpose of rubrics is to slot students into a category. By now, it should be clear that the kind of assessment that I am advocating is more concerned with helping students learn than it is with finding a slot in which to put them.

> A rubric is a particular format for criteria—it is a written down version of the criteria, with all score points described and defined. The best rubrics are worded in a way that covers the essence of what teachers look for when they judge quality and they reflect the best thinking in the field about what constitutes good performance.
>
> —Arter and McTighe (2001)

Rubrics can be useful tools for teachers, students, and parents. They are more than just evaluation tools to use at the end of instruction; they help clarify instructional goals and serve as teaching targets (Arter & McTighe, 2001). All too often, educators see rubrics as replacements for grading categories. Instead of recognizing that the power of rubrics is as mechanisms for making performance criteria visible, they transform the descriptions into the number designations. A student is quickly labeled as a "2" or a "3." The end result is counterproductive. A useful tool for learning becomes another sorting mechanism, and the value that it might have added to learning and teaching disappears.

Sometimes a rubric, even a good one, is not enough. Royce Sadler (1989) wrote a landmark paper describing why students need to have visible images of what excellence looks like. This knowledge of excellence develops progressively through a series of cognitive tacking maneuvers. Criteria and descriptions offer reference points along the way, but there is no substitute for "seeing" excellence. There is no one model of excellence for any area. Many of them exist, and students need to see (or hear, or imagine) what these various images of excellence are like.

When students are striving toward a difficult goal, especially one that is complex and requires the integration of new learning and a number of different skills, they benefit from seeing how it looks when it's done and from the process that an expert went through to get there. Having an image of where they are going, how long it takes to get there, and what the stages look like both motivates and provides targets that students can visualize and strive for along the way.

Think about athletes as they perfect and extend their performances. Personal video cameras have become essential tools for them as they watch the way that recognized experts do it, videotape their own performance, and make adjustments to fine-tune their own style so that it is more effective. The footage of experts in action provides targets for changes, but the individual athletes consider what they see in relation to their own body type and what they already do well to enhance their performance, rather than just emulating the expert.

"The Case of the Brass Band"

A music teacher in a small, rural secondary school, himself an accomplished trumpet player who played swing music with a brass band, offered an extracurricular program in the school for students who wanted to learn to play brass instruments. He made an announcement to the school that the "band" would meet after school on Tuesdays. Anyone in the school could come. The only requirement was that the students attend every session and practice in between. His promise to them: "We'll perform for the school at the spring concert. And you'll be great."

He was surprised and delighted that more than 20 people showed up at the first after-school class, including one teacher who "used to play the trombone" and the junior custodian, who played drums with a rock band and thought he might be able to add something to the group. The music teacher gave the motley crew an initial pep talk:

> We're all in this together. A band can only work as a whole group. So, each of us has to learn alone and learn together so that we can make the music work. Here's how we're going to

do it. Today, I want you to listen to some big band music, and we'll talk about what you like or don't like about each piece. I'll introduce you to the instruments and let you hear how each of them sounds and see how they work. I have copies of the tapes you're going to hear so you can take them home and listen to them again. When we meet next week, we'll decide who is going to play which instruments and what pieces we want to start with. You can take an instrument with you this week as well, if you think you know the instrument that you want. Or you can come in after school and try out any ones that you want.

This initial statement set the tone for the rest of the big band program. Everyone eventually selected an instrument, and the group agreed about the selections that it wanted to learn. From there, the real work began. The routines of the weekly class were straightforward. In early sessions, they involved the following:

- Listening to the segment of the piece that they were working on, using the recording

- Practicing the segment as a group

- Practicing individually (those members of the band identified by the teacher as doing something well)

- Giving feedback to these individuals based on a simple PMI (plus, minus, interesting)

- Listening to a recording of the particular instrument alone

- Analyzing the recordings in relation to the individual performances, with discussion about what is essential for a good performance, especially within a group, and what is unique to the particular performer

After each session, the teacher identified several students to meet with him during the week. Before they came for their private session, the students practiced a segment that they were finding particularly challenging and taped their playing while they were practicing. They brought three of these taped performances to the private session, and the teacher worked with them to help them "hear" their playing and to make adjustments. Once the session was over, the students received several tapes by experts on the instrument, performing the same piece, often very differently from one another. Their homework task was to analyze and describe what the different artists did that was similar and what was different, and to try to introduce some of these elements into their own playing.

As time went on, each student performed solo for the complete group, not as the perfect performance, but as a phase in the process of learning and creating the final production. The explicit expectation was that the group would provide helpful and challenging feedback to the individual about the performance as a solo, and as part of the band, so that the composition would work as a whole. The teacher used his considerable talent along the way to write (and rewrite) new arrangements for different individuals and different instruments. He even found a place for a big band drummer that built on the talents of the rock band drummer.

The final production was an enormous success, but that was the least important element in this lesson about learning. The students in this group learned that

- There is no single right answer;

- You get better when you practice, if you know what to practice and how to make it better;

- What sounds like confusing noise in the beginning can be taken apart and understood, and when it's put back together, you can hear the differences;

- When you can hear (or see) where you are headed, it's easier to get there;

- When you work together, you can create something that is bigger than any single person can on his or her own.

Ideas, Connections, and Extensions (ICE)

Young and Wilson (2000, p. 2) describe an approach to assessment that they call the ICE approach, which teachers can use "on the run" in classrooms. It is a portable technique for assessing growth that is generalizable across students, subjects, ages, and levels of schooling. I think that it offers a valuable organizer for teachers as they consider structuring instruction and feedback in their classes. ICE is described in Table 9.3.

These authors have found that the ICE approach makes sense and is manageable for teachers as they juggle all of the activities that make up their busy days. In fact, it serves as an organizer to keep them on track and focused on learning and individual students.

Table 9.3   ICE Approach to Assessment of Growth

ICE means	Description	Evidence
Ideas	*Ideas* are the building blocks of learning: the steps in a process, the necessary vocabulary, and the introductory skills that form the basis of learning. Sometimes, they are the bits of information in notes and textbooks; sometimes, they are steps in a process; sometimes, they are guidelines for action.	Students convey • The fundamentals • The basic facts • Vocabulary/definitions • Details • Elemental concepts
Connections	*Connections* are the relationships and patterns that exist between and among ideas and with previous knowledge and ideas. Novices follow prescriptions and manuals. Experts see patterns and can take shortcuts because they understand the underlying connections to other ideas.	Students communicate • The relationship or connections among the basic concepts • A relationship or connection between the new ideas and what they already know
Extensions	*Extensions* are the final stage in growth of learning and occur when individuals no longer need to refer to the rules for operations and no longer make conscious connections among the bits or even to their own experience. They have internalized the learning so much that it helps to define them as people. Rules have been abandoned for "maxims," or portable truths that have meaning even if they are not expressed.	Students show that relationships are internalized by • Using new knowledge in novel and creative ways to extend ideas or concepts, often well beyond the original learning context • Answering the hypothetical questions, "What does this mean? How does this shape my view of the world?"

SOURCE: Adapted from Young and Wilson (2000).

Ideas for Follow-Up

1. Make an ICE chart for a unit that you are teaching. Identify the ideas, connections, and extensions that make up the unit. Create assessment tasks that allow you to ascertain students' facility with the ideas, connections, and extensions.

2. Work as a team to consider student work and decide what kinds of feedback prompts you would use. Remember to identify the concept or skill that is the focus of the exercise before you begin.

CHAPTER **10**

Using Assessment for Reflection and Self-Monitoring

As I pointed out earlier, learning is an active process of constructing thoughts and making sense of the world around us. Ideas are the raw material for this process, and existing knowledge and beliefs can enable or impede new learning. Learning is also dependent on self-monitoring and awareness. We all decide when and how to use various skills; we check what we believe to be true against socially and culturally determined norms, and we continually decide how reasonable the resulting formulation feels. Effective learners develop cognitive routines for organizing, synthesizing, and reorganizing ideas. They also engage in self-monitoring and provide themselves with feedback that leads to the emergence of new ideas, combinations, or patterns.

> Assumption: Everyone can be an expert at something, sometime.

"The Case of Jojo"

When she was about 5 years old, my niece Joanna (Jojo to the family) came up to me and announced that "All cats are girls, and all dogs are boys." When I asked her why she believed cats were girls and dogs were boys, she responded, "Your cat *Molly* is a girl, and she's little and smooth. Girls are little and smooth, too. Cats are girls. The dog next door is a boy, and he's big and rough, just like boys are big and rough. Dogs are boys." Clearly, she had identified a problem, surveyed her environment, gathered data, and formulated a hypothesis. When she tested it, it held. Pretty sophisticated logic.

100

I pulled a book about dogs from my bookshelf and showed her a picture of a chihuahua.

"What's this?" I asked.

"Dog," she replied.

"Girl or boy?"

"It's a boy, dogs are boys."

"But it's little and smooth," I pointed out.

"Sometimes, they can be little and smooth," said Jojo.

I turned to a picture of an Irish Setter, surrounded by puppies. She was perturbed.

"What's this?"

"Dog," she replied, with some hesitation.

"Boy or girl?"

After a long pause, she said, "Maybe it's the dad." But she didn't look convinced, and she quickly asked, "Can dogs be girls, Aunt Lorna?"

This anecdote is a simple but vivid demonstration of the process of reflection and self-monitoring that we all use when we are trying to make sense of the world around us. Jojo had a conception of what she wanted to know (the gender of cats and dogs). She had come to a conclusion based on her initial investigation. With the intervention of a teacher (me), who gave her the wherewithal to compare her conceptions with other examples in the real world, she was able to see the gap between her understanding and other evidence. Once she had the new knowledge, she moved quickly to adjust her view and consider alternative perspectives.

Students as Their Own Best Assessors

We want students to become self-starting and self-motivated lifelong learners. If they are to become critical thinkers and problem solvers who can bring their talents and their knowledge to bear on their decisions and actions, they have to develop skills of self-assessment and self-adjustment. They can't just wait for someone to tell them the right answer. At this stage, all of the ideas that have emerged in other chapters come back into play as important factors in the work of learning. They include the following:

- Engaging students in the real work of learning is motivation at its best.

- Clear goals and visible examples of what "good work looks like," when it's done and while it's in process, set the stage.

- Student involvement in determining the goals, learning methods, and decisions about success increases their self-awareness and helps them see errors, consider alternatives, and make adjustments.

- Diagnostic assessment provides teachers with guides to share with their students.

- Descriptive feedback makes the next step manageable while providing maximum independence.

- Sharing the decision making and giving students practice in monitoring their own work gives them confidence and competence in making important judgments about their learning and their decisions.

- Bringing parents and peers into the process adds allies and co-conspirators to the learning process.

Developing Self-Evaluation Habits of Mind

A number of writers have referred to the "habits of mind" that creative, critical, and self-regulated thinkers use and that students (and many adults, for that matter) need to develop. These habits are ways of thinking that will enable students to learn on their own, whatever they want or need to know at any point in their lives (Marzano, Pickering, & McTighe, 1993).

> We must constantly remind ourselves that the ultimate purpose of evaluation is to enable students to evaluate themselves. Educators may have been practicing this skill to the exclusion of the learners. We need to shift part of this responsibility to students. Fostering students' ability to direct and redirect themselves must be a major goal—or what is education for?
>
> —Costa (1989)

When people succeed or fail, they can explain their success or failure to themselves in various ways: effort, ability, task factors, or luck. Only the first of these attributions is likely to promote adaptive motivational tendencies. The student can decide to try harder and be successful. The other explanations—ability, task difficulty, or luck—are all out of the student's control. When students do not believe that they have control over their achievements, they are not motivated to work in school.

In particular, several authors have identified an "inquiry habit of mind" as an essential component of profitable learning for individuals and groups (Earl & Lee, 1998; Katz, Sutherland, & Earl, in press; Newmann, 1996; Wiggins, 1993). If students are going to develop these "habits of mind" and become inquiry-minded, they need to experience continuous, genuine success. They need to feel as if they are in an environment where it is safe to take chances and where feedback and support are readily available and challenging. This does not mean the absence of failure. It means using their habits of mind to identify misconceptions and inaccuracies and to work with them toward a more complete and coherent understanding. Teachers have the responsibility of creating environments for students to become confident, competent self-assessors who monitor their own learning.

> I look at losing as research, not failure.
>
> —Billie-Jean King (tennis star)

Emotional Safety

Becoming independent and responsible learners who embrace assessment as a positive part of the process is not something that comes easily. In fact, it is downright scary for many adults, let alone young people. So don't be surprised if some (perhaps many) students do not wholeheartedly embrace the idea. The extent to which students are willing to engage in self-assessment is very much connected to their sense of self and their self-esteem. Persistence depends on expectations of success, even if they are not immediate. Students who have had a history of failure experiences or who fear failure will adopt techniques to protect themselves, even if it means avoiding opportunities for learning. Students who define themselves by their ability are often dependent on high grades as a visible symbol of their worth and find the challenge of moving away from their positions of confidence rather like a free fall into the unknown. It isn't enough to have a few safe moments or

> Emotional safety is necessary for intellectual risk taking.
>
> —Gipps et al. (2000)

episodes of learning. They need to be the norm. Through detailed case studies of individual children throughout their primary schooling, Pollard and Filer (1999) demonstrate how these students continuously shaped their identities and actively evolved as they moved from one classroom context to the next. What this means is that each student's sense of self as a pupil can be enhanced or threatened by changes in their relationships over time, structural position in the classroom, and relative success or failure. It was particularly affected by their teachers' expectations, learning and teaching strategies, classroom organization, and criteria for evaluation. This work shows how important the teacher is to students' sense of self and their views of themselves in school.

Lots of Examples of "What Good Work Looks Like"

Although curriculum guides and standards provide a skeleton image of the expectations for students, nothing is as powerful as multiple images of "what it looks like when experts do it." Not only do students begin to see and hear and feel the expectations for the work at hand, they become acutely aware of the variations that can occur and the legitimacy of those variations. Even in courses like mathematics, there are examples of the elegance and precision that come when experts understand the underlying principles and can apply formulas as shorthand mechanisms for solving problems. In the pool table examples, the students who moved from counting to pattern identification to algebraic notation as a symbolic representation of the relationships "saw" the way the patterns worked. They acquired "expertise" that they could transfer to new situations. The students who did not see the patterns needed more examples and practice with concrete activities to move to the next step. Although the students may never reach or even aspire to the heights of the experts in an area, seeing what the subject allows can have a value of its own. Students of art or music or literature are inspired by the work of masters in the field; students of geography or science or computer programming can be as well.

Once students have a sense of where they are aiming, teachers can offer many intermediate examples of the stages along the way and how experts struggle as well to meet their own expectations. I recently saw a senior English writing textbook that included images of the handwritten pages that author Margaret Atwood had written in the beginning stages of a new novel. One of the pages was messy, often illegible, with lots of words crossed out and marginal notes all over it. In a later chapter, the same page was displayed, now in a computer file, still with many ideas jumbled and half completed, and with lots of notes to herself in brackets. Near the end of the book, the same selection was shown as it appeared in the final manuscript—a very different piece from when it began. Students were using these artifacts to analyze how Atwood was thinking and why she was making the changes that she made, and they were practicing the kind of analysis that they could bring to their own thinking and writing in progress.

Real Involvement and Responsibility

When teachers work to involve students and promote their independence, they are really teaching students to be responsible for their own learning and giving them the tools to undertake it wisely and well. How else are they likely to develop the self-regulatory skills that are the hallmark of experts? It isn't likely, however, that students will become competent, realistic self-evaluators on their own. They need to be taught skills of self-assessment, have routine and challenging opportunities to practice, and develop internal feedback or self-monitoring mechanisms to validate and call into question their own judgments. For students to become independent learners, they need to develop a complicated combination of skills, attitudes, and dispositions. These don't emerge unaided; they are taught and developed over time, like any other complex set of skills. "The Case of Choices" that follows in this chapter is an excellent example of building independence, not only in specific tasks, but in life. Experts may have begun with some exceptional talents that gave them a head start, but they have had to learn the rest by setting goals, organizing their thinking and their lives, self-monitoring, and self-correcting. Each of these skills can be learned, not by posting them up as rules but from helping students engage in setting goals, organizing their world (in small pieces at first), monitoring their progress, and changing their plans based on what they learn, over and over again, during their years in school.

Recording and Reporting for Learning

Integrating new ideas in a discipline with what the students know, and using these new ideas to inform their learning, requires a different kind of recordkeeping and reporting. Instead of dedicating their recording and reporting time to a small number of "marking" and "report card" days, teachers will find that they need to make notes and keep records daily, sometimes on the fly, sometimes in a more orderly fashion. Recording becomes more descriptive, rather than judgmental. What did Jose do? What prompts did I use with Jesse? What artifacts show growth over time? Students become the prime clients for the data that are accumulating, not as statements of their value but as milestones in their learning.

Targeted Feedback

When feedback allows students to see the gap between their actual production and some reference point that makes sense to them, they are both motivated and able to work with their conceptions and make adjustments. The work of teachers is to provide current, accurate, and focused feedback, with examples and reasonable directions for the student to keep going. Informal feedback can refocus students' thinking and allow them to collect their thoughts and feelings so that they can carry on with less frustration and confusion. The examples that occur to me range from a teacher stopping to ask a formative question to class discussions where ideas are shared and challenged by the group.

More formal feedback for self-evaluation occurs when students meet with teachers to discuss where they are and where they are going, and to negotiate the procedures to get there. These less frequent and formal opportunities can provide chances to regroup, establish new or reaffirm existing skills if necessary, and come back to try again with renewed vigor and additional strategies.

Discussion, Challenge, and Reflection

Ideas are not transported ready-made into students' minds. As the Jojo story showed, new ideas emerge through careful consideration and reasoned analysis, and just as important, through interaction with text, pictures, and people. Learning is not private, and it isn't silent. It may happen in individual minds, but it is constantly connected to the world outside and the people in that world. Peers and parents can be strong advocates and contributors to this process, not as judges, meting out marks or favors, but as participants in this process of analysis, comparison, rethinking, and reinforcing that makes up learning. Consider activities like "fishbowls," where a few students discuss a problem and their analysis of it while the rest of the class sits in a circle around them, making notes of ideas, competing hypotheses, resources that might be useful, and suggestions for next steps. At the end of the discussion, the students from the circle write their ideas on sticky notes, and the fishbowl students take them and organize them as a starting point for their next discussion on the issue. Learning is a social activity. Peers and parents, when they understand their role and the situation is structured to support the process, can be key players as students grapple with what they believe to be true in relation to the views, perspectives, and challenges of others.

Practice, Practice, Practice

Like any other complex skill, self-evaluation is hard work that requires commitment and practice to become automatic. This usually necessitates trying something again and again, working at it, feeling uncomfortable for a while, and experiencing new responses.

"The Case of Choices"

In a secondary school in which I have worked, the staff decided that they would try to make the transition to secondary school more humane by keeping the ninth-grade students together as a group and working to bring some coherence to their program. The timetable was based on 70-minute periods, and the students traveled to each class as a group. The core program for the semester was mathematics, English, computer applications, and French. The students were being taught by four teachers who planned together and sometimes team-taught. Let me describe one day that I spent with them.

The day began like most secondary school days—the students were in their homeroom classrooms for attendance checks, announcements, and opening activities, all undercut by a din of whispers and sounds of people moving. I arrived with one of the teachers (Mr. Math) and sat at the back of his classroom. It struck me that this was no ordinary secondary school classroom. There were things on the walls: displays of students' work, a poster containing the expectations from the mathematics curriculum document. On a side table sat calculators (regular and graphing), manipulatives, resource books, and several computers. One corner of the room contained a round table surrounded by games, puzzles, and cards, some commercial, some homemade. As the announcements ended, the teacher began the class with a review of the "bellringer." He had gone into the class early and put open-ended mathematics questions on each of the tables (shared by four students) in the room. The whispering that I had heard was the students discussing the bellringer of the day. The question of the day was based on a current event in the community. There had been a hot-air balloon festival on the weekend, and several balloons were taking passengers up for rides. The question was, "How many people do you think went up in the hot air balloons over the weekend? Why?" The resource for the exercise was the morning newspaper, which had a story about the event that included an estimate of the number of people who attended and gave some details about size, capacity, and so on. The question did not have a "right" answer. The ensuing discussion included hypothesis generation, estimation, calculations, logic, debate, and attention to evidence. The amazing thing was that most of it happened before class started. The review was quick. Each table had a reporter who described the students' thinking and conclusions. The group voted on the best one, based on the quality of the arguments, and the winning table took a bow.

Later in the day, I went with these students to their computer applications class. Most of the students were sitting at the computers

> We have so much to gain by admitting students to the "secret garden" of assessment to empower them to direct and manage their own learning.
>
> —Broadfoot (2002)

working on spreadsheets, entering data, and calculating mortgage payments based on different interest rates and amortization periods. As I walked around, I realized that one group of five or six students was sitting in a corner working on something else. The students had their French text out and were clearly not doing spreadsheets. When I approached, I was surprised that the text was not whisked away. Instead, they continued, asking each other French vocabulary questions, seemingly oblivious to my presence. When I asked what they were doing, the answer was straightforward: "Studying for the French test next period."

"But what about the mortgage assignment?" I asked.

"Oh, we'll do that after school. We've chosen to spend this time on French," said a charming young woman, who then took me by the arm away from her hard-working peers and explained that their teachers believed in choices. At the beginning of the year, the teachers had told them that life was all about choices. "Outside of school, people don't tell you what to do every minute, and bells don't ring to tell you to do something else." So, the students were expected to make choices and then to live with the consequences. The teachers had talked about the curriculum in the four subjects for the semester and showed them how the assignments and classes would help them learn what they needed to know. The expectations were displayed on the classroom walls. Classes continued on the regular timetable. But students were responsible for their own choices about what they did and when. The teachers gave all of the students diaries so that they could organize their own time and helped them decide how to use the diaries to schedule and plan. Every day, a few students met with their homeroom teacher to review their plans and their progress and to make adjustments. When students didn't do their work, they weren't punished. They were reminded that they were responsible for their own decisions. But it was clear that they had made a choice to neglect their studies and that there would be consequences. Ultimately, of course, the consequence could be failing to achieve the requirements for completion of the course. Remember, this was school.

When I met with the teachers at the end of the day, I raised this issue of choices. For them, it was clear. "How else will they learn to make reasonable decisions if we don't teach them and then let them do it in an environment where there are limits and they are safe?" said one. "Sure," added another, "some students don't want to be more responsible for their learning. They are very happy to be receptacles for the 'stuff' of the course and discard it when the time is up and the test is done. That's not good enough for us. If someone is resistant, we need to find out what he's afraid of and find the right scaffolds to make it safe to take tiny risks."

Self-monitoring and self-adjustment protect students from the vagaries of the world around them. This group of teachers was determined to help the students develop and practice the habits of mind that would serve them in the future.

Ideas for Follow-Up

1.   Use a fishbowl technique in your study group. Each of you should come prepared to discuss the ways in which you use assessment to encourage students' self-reflection. The rest of the group listens intently and serves as a "critical friend," asking probing questions and offering constructive suggestions.

2.   Brainstorm as many ways as you can that teachers (and students) can record information about ongoing learning and use it to inform the next stage of learning.

CHAPTER 11

Using Assessment for Optimum Learning

Assessment is, and will continue to be, contentious in both public and political arenas. Moving toward assessment for and as learning will require educators to have courage and stamina, as well as motivation and capacity. This chapter is about how to get there. It has been written for teachers to stimulate thinking, challenge ideas, and inspire action.

In case anyone doubts it, considerable research evidence shows that teachers make a difference in students' learning (Wenglinsky, 2002). Although background characteristics do have an influence, they can be moderated and even overcome by high-quality, active teachers who press all of their students to grow, regardless of their backgrounds; adjust their classroom activities to accommodate the multiple levels of abstraction of the students; and engage students in their learning. Classroom assessment can be a powerful tool for teachers in their pursuit of high-quality learning for their students.

The good news is that teachers intuitively trust their own classroom assessments, prefer them to other assessment methods, and already use them for both instructional purposes and determination of students' grades (Rogers, 1991; Stiggins, 1994). Unless they are under close public scrutiny, schools and teachers pay little attention to externally imposed tests and go about their own business, using classroom assessment for their judgments. They believe that their own assessments and observations are direct, unmediated, and inherently valid, unlike external tests, which, they argue, are indirect, mediated, and inherently invalid (Broadfoot, 1994; Wilson, 1994).

The bad news is that teachers' trust in their assessment practices is not always justified, and the classroom assessments that teachers trust don't always promote learning. Assessment interacts with learning; the interaction can be a forward one to reflect and support learning goals or a backward one that diverts attention from learning or sets up barriers in the learning process. As Black (1998) says:

• Classroom evaluation practices generally encourage superficial and rote learning, concentrating on recall of isolated details, usually items of knowledge.

• Teachers do not generally review the assessment questions that they use and they don't discuss them critically with peers, so there is little reflection on what is being assessed.

• The grading function is over-emphasized and the learning function is under-emphasized.

• There is a tendency to use a normative rather than a criterion approach that emphasizes competition between pupils rather than personal improvement of each. (p. 111)

Changing assessment to reflect some of the principles included in this volume will be a challenge for teachers. They receive little information about assessment in teacher training, and when they do, the focus is often on Assessment *of* Learning for grading purposes. Their own histories and experiences have been the same. The process of assessment in most classrooms is a game (or battle), with teachers pitted against

> Assumption: Teachers' overriding moral purpose is to meet the needs of students, even when it conflicts with personal preferences.

students. There are some explicit rules (e.g., no cheating, attendance at classes counts for 15%, etc.) and many implicit ones (e.g., teachers have the power to decide) in this game. Teachers create secret tests. Students try to imagine (guess) what the tests will include. Marking is a private affair, done late at night in rooms lit only by late-night television screens. Grade books are essential elements in the teacher's arsenal, giving the proof (or at least the illusion) of objectivity, precision, and accuracy. Even the idea of sharing the assessment process with students raises suspicion and challenges the teachers' position in the classroom.

Penetrating the myths and the realities about classroom assessment will be challenging. Assessment has never been straightforward or rational, or even very objective (no matter how neat and tidy the marking schemes and grade books look). It is a deeply personal and emotional experience for the students being assessed, the students' parents, and, often, the teacher (Earl & LeMahieu, 1997). It is spontaneous, idiosyncratic, unpredictable, context-dependent, time-bound, and group-influenced, and it leads to different responses depending on the student involved (Wilson, 1994). It is also constrained by the state, district, and school policies that require particular kinds of reporting or attach rewards or sanctions to student grades (Darling-Hammond, 1994). But these are not reasons to abandon classroom assessment and replace it with external assessment procedures. These are precisely the reasons why classroom assessment is so important and why changing it is worth doing—because it matters in students' lives.

Making radical changes to classroom assessment is risky business. Regardless of the dangers, this is not the time for timidity. Teachers have the chance to take charge of change and reformulate the nature of assessment and even of accountability in education. Once again, I have a preferred future. Assessment can become an instrument of learning. Accountability can be diverted from the accounting that emerges from large-scale assessment and external control to its rightful place in schools, as a conversation between educational professionals and those whom they serve—students and parents (Earl & LeMahieu, 1997). The evidence of success will be obvious and visible examples of learning, not through disembodied scores and league tables, but through the accomplishments of young people in their schooling and their lives.

In the rest of this chapter, I examine some of the things that educators can do to prepare for this future. None of them is prescriptive. Instead, they are designed to offer ways of thinking about the purpose of schools; the role that we, as educators, play in schools; and the challenges that we face if we hope to transform schools for students who will live the bulk of their lives in the 21st century.

Think About What You Believe to Be True

The changes in assessment that this volume advocates require some dramatic shifts in thinking. Don't forget—the belief systems and images of schooling that most of us hold come from our own history of learning and schooling. We are products of a factory model of schools and a culture dominated by Assessment *of* Learning. Changing attitudes and beliefs that have been with us for a lifetime is not easy. Watkins et al. (2001) suggest that everyone is in a constant state of consciousness and competence in relation to his or her learning in any area. The authors describe four possible states (see Table 11.1). It seems to me that it is important to revisit this matrix routinely

Table 11.1   Four Possible States of the Learner

	Unconscious of need to learn a specific skill or knowledge	*Conscious of need to learn a specific skill or knowledge*
Incompetent in relation to a specific skill or knowledge	I don't know that I don't know how to do it.	I know that I don't know how to do it.
Competent in relation to a specific skill or knowledge	I can do it but I'm not aware how.	I know how to do it and am aware of how I am doing it.

SOURCE: Watkins et al. (2001).

and decide which quadrant is the best representation, at present, of personal learning.

Beliefs About Learning and Teaching

As long as teachers assume that the "stuff of learning" is the content in texts and other resources, that teaching is transmitting that "stuff" to students, and that student learning either happens or it doesn't, it is unlikely that much will change in schools. Learning, as I describe it in Chapter 4, is an active and demanding process for students.

Beliefs About Assessment

Researchers who have been working with teachers committed to changing their assessment practices are finding that teachers have difficulty moving away from practices that are so ingrained that they have never even questioned them before. They believe that their testing has to be a formal, objective process that is uniformly administered and separate from teaching (Bliem & Davinroy, 1997, cited in Shepard, 2000; Torrance, 2001). Even when they engage in formative assessment, they often see it as extracting a product from students that they can then use for planning of teaching. This is a far cry from a process of consistently using assessment data to plan and respond on the fly to adapt teaching to the needs of their students and to promote student self-assessment. The first stage toward new practices (as is always the case in learning) is an awareness of personal enduring beliefs.

Learn About Learning

If schools are for learning, then knowing about learning for teachers is like knowing about anatomy for doctors. You have to know all there is to know. Unlike anatomy, there is a tremendous amount of new knowledge about learning, and more still to be discovered. We are still far from a complete understanding of how the mind works and how this complex human process of learning takes place. For teachers, this makes learning about learning an ongoing professional responsibility in order to do the job well. Focusing on the tools of teaching without an understanding of learning is short-sighted. Learning needs to come first.

Know Your Subject

Using assessment to guide students in their learning demands a great deal of expertise from teachers. Not only do they need to update their own organizational mental models with new knowledge in their subject discipline(s), some of which renders old knowledge obsolete, but they also have to have a deep and detailed understanding of the way that knowledge development typically happens in their discipline. Knowing what feedback to give assumes an understanding of what causes errors and a recognition of strategies to bring students face-to-face with their misconceptions in ways that make it difficult to continue to hold their existing views.

One of the most compelling and surprising findings in our evaluation of the National Literacy and Numeracy Strategies in England (Earl, Fullan, Leithwood, & Watson, 2000) has been the shallow subject knowledge on the part of the teachers. This is consistent with the findings of Cohen and Hill (2001) in their research on mathematics in California. Although teachers may have a command of the subject themselves, they often do not have the knowledge of the way that they learned it, and more important, how others have learned it or have stumbled along the way. Teachers need to be able to ask the right questions at the right time, anticipate conceptual pitfalls, and have at the ready a repertoire of tasks that will help students take the next steps. This requires a deep knowledge of subject matter. Imagine all that the teacher in "The Bog" example needed to know about early language development and the kinds of misconceptions and confusions she might anticipate in the children's work. In her analysis, she was not looking for right or wrong answers in the students' writing. She was looking for evidence (or the absence of evidence) about the kind of thinking in which Jonathon was engaged. She was trying to make his learning visible so that she could intervene and assist.

The same is true for "The Pool Table." It is only because the teacher has a deep and flexible understanding of the principles that underlie algebraic notation and logic that he was able to devise an open-ended task that engaged all of the students and gave him invaluable information about their thinking and preconceptions. From there, of course, he was able to move quickly to establish the next activities for individuals and groups that would challenge each one of them without leaving them floundering.

So, knowing your subject deeply and intimately is critical—not just the content but the conventions, structures, organizers, underlying concepts, standard and nonstandard procedures, typical misconceptions and misunderstandings, and whatever else makes the subject what it is.

Be an Expert Teacher

Pedagogical understanding is about putting the understanding of learning and content knowledge together with a repertoire of strategies and resources for effective teaching. Expert teachers know about learning and the subjects that they teach, and they have a deep knowledge of pedagogy. They are constantly applying what they know in these areas to the diversity in students' strengths, weaknesses, home background, cultural experiences, developmental stage, and learning styles that exists in their classroom context. Watching an expert teacher is like watching a master jazz musician. The core phrases remain constant, but the treatment, diversions, embellishments, and pacing are variable and flexible, dictated by the other musicians and the context. The product may be unpredictable; it is always complex; and it can touch the souls of very diverse listeners.

I had the fortune for several months to observe such a teacher regularly. In an interview, he described a unit of work that I was observing in his Grade 8 class this way:

> This class is really musical. So I chose *A Tale of Two Cities* to study in novel study. We went to see *Les Misérables* at the theatre and watched it on video, too. That brought us to social studies. We focused on the politics and social structures of the time. We had an in-depth talk about the justice systems in England and France and compared them and talked about why they were different from one another. Each group in the class is doing a project connected to one of the key themes in the novel. They are really great. One group is even writing an operetta.

As an observer in the class, I watched him work with individuals and groups during this unit. They were all approaching their agreed-upon tasks in different ways, using different resources. Some were writing critical reviews of *Les Misérables* for the school newspaper. Others were composing an epic poem about the plight of the poor. Of course, the operetta was in progress. One boy had decided that he wanted to work individually to compare the current Canadian justice system to the English and French ones that they had studied to see what had endured (given that Canada was originally settled by both cultures and remains an amalgam of the two) and speculate about why.

At the same time as these children were engaged in dramatically different activities, the learning expectations from the provincial curriculum were posted around the room. A poster board contained a web organizer centered on the expectations on which they were working in this unit. The whole class had participated in deciding which expectations they were going to address and what the prerequisite skills and knowledge would be to get there. Finally, each child or group had a small whiteboard on which the teacher had written the detailed expectations on which the particular individual or group was focusing during this part of the unit.

The students were busy and engaged in their work. The teacher (sometimes hard to spot as he moved around the active and jam-packed classroom) used his time giving on-the-spot directions, asking questions, providing support, identifying possible resources, challenging thinking, and supplying focused feedback. When the recess bell rang, most of the students continued with their work until they finished the immediate task. When they returned from their exercise break, they went back to it. The teacher was in the hallway, with me, considering the displays from the prior unit that adorned the walls.

Work Together

For some time, collaboration among teachers has been touted as a major contributor to effective schools and the improvement of schools (Fullan & Hargreaves, 1992). Assessment and learning are a natural focus for discussion among teachers. In fact, working together and reaching some shared decisions are essential if teachers are truly committed to using assessment for and as learning in schools and providing consistency and coherence for student learning over time and across grades. Talking with each other is the first stage of sharing interpretations of curriculum and expectations for students and giving teachers a chance to see the connections in and across the curriculum. They have to develop the big picture as a road map for the journeys that they will take with the students in the school, not just for the single semester or year that they have direct responsibility for a group, but for the duration of the students' time in school.

As teachers struggle with the challenge of providing descriptions of their students' learning, they find themselves doubting their judgment and suggestions. These doubts are no different from what teachers have experienced for years. They ask themselves questions such as, "How sure am I that I'm right?" and "How much confidence do I have that I'm giving a fair and accurate picture of this student?" One of the most powerful ways to gain confidence in assessment decisions is to share them. After working with a group of teachers that was engaged in the tough process of mapping expectations for students across several grades and subjects, I received a letter from one of them saying,

> Just wanted to let you know that we had our first parents' night this week and it was awesome. We showed them our charts (posted in the hall) and we talked about how the integrated units will work during the term. It felt really good to be able to show where the different skills were being addressed (including spelling) and to get them excited about the theme units as well. The best part was when I met with parents of my kids. I felt as if I could speak with some authority. It wasn't just me and the kids' work speaking. I could hear the group's voices in my head.

When teachers involve students in their own assessment, the need for whole-school approaches, as well as consistency and progression in targets, becomes even more obvious. As students move from one class to another across years or across subjects, it is essential that the opportunity for involvement be continued and that they see the way the learning intentions change, grow, and become more sophisticated. Otherwise, students are likely to be confused and suspicious of the system that changes the rules on such fundamental issues on a whim.

In a delightful book called *The Competent Classroom,* by Allison Zmuda and Mary Tomaino (2001), the authors describe their collaborative journey of aligning high school curriculum, standards, and assessment. They worked together to challenge each other and to hone and refine their skills as teachers. They found that a change in assessment strategies affected everything else, so they needed to make multiple adjustments. Their journey took them through discussing "essential questions" to guide the program, aligning curricular goals with their essential questions, developing and refining content standards and instructional objectives, bringing assessments into the mix, actually implementing a project, and using standards and assessments to calculate grades. Their vivid description of the process, with all its difficulties, is a wonderful example of planning at its best and collaboration that results in something bigger and better than either one could have created alone—collaboration that includes assessment of, for, and as learning.

Be Gentle With Yourself, But Don't Give Up

Even when teachers are willing to change and interested in changing their assessment practices, they find that it is not as easy as they thought it would be. Changing beliefs, practices, and habits is hard and frustrating. I liken it to using a seat belt in a car. When I learned to drive, seat belts were not mandatory. I learned to get in the car, start the engine, check where I was going, and drive away. When seatbelts became standard requirements, new drivers learned to get in the car, buckle up, and then start the engine. To this day, I follow my old habits, and I'm constantly scrambling to fasten the seat belt as I pull away. If my new car had a mechanism that meant the engine would not start until I buckled the belt, I would have the motivation to do it—I certainly know how to do it—and I would still spend the first few weeks (hopefully not months) cursing all and sundry when I got in and reverted to the old routine. If something this straightforward takes so much energy, thought, and practice, why would we ever assume that changing how we teach will be easy?

A good deal of research on the impact of professional development has demonstrated how difficult it is for teachers to actually implement new strategies (Joyce & Showers, 1982). Changing practices takes time and practice—time to construct an understanding of all of the ways that assessment can contribute to learning, and practice with new skills and approaches. It is likely that teachers will be faced with the prospect of adopting a whole new way of teaching and casting aside or unlearning much of what they have known and done confidently before. This requires a significant amount of practice and lots of scope for making mistakes. A classically trained violinist faced with a new piece composed for jazz fiddle is likely to have to practice harder to master the different rhythms and dynamics. An artist like Seurat would have developed his pointillist method through much trial and error and refinement of technique. Many of the artist's drawings and sketches hanging in exhibitions are practice attempts. Similarly, the play at the theatre has gone through a rehearsal period, and the rehearsal comes after the actors and actresses have already devoted significant time and a range of strategies to learning their lines (Stoll et al., 2002).

Self-Monitoring and Self-Development for You, Too

So, efficient and lifelong learning is about making connections, adding new ideas, organizing and reorganizing understanding, and, ultimately, self-monitoring and self-correction or adjustment. We've come full circle. As I said in Chapter 4,

> Learning is at the core of our being, as individuals and collectively. It is the key to equipping future generations to respond and survive in a frenetically and unpredictably changing world. We have not even approached the limits of what can be learned.

Using assessment for optimum learning for students is a process of growth, change, monitoring, and more change for teachers, along with their students. We are asking students to be brave, take risks, and learn more and better. We face the same challenge. Teachers need to understand their own learning and internalize learning habits of mind as well. This means showing students that you are a learner as well, and having a willingness to engage in in-depth explorations of your own learning—what motivates and influences it, what hinders it, and what it feels like to be on that learning curve. Even those teachers who are well

> For teachers, going to school must be as much about learning as it is about teaching. They must have time each day to learn, plan lessons, critique student work, and support improvement as members of learning teams. . . . Staff development cannot be something educators do only on specified days in the school calendar. It must be part of every educator's daily work schedule.
>
> —Hirsch (2001)

on the road to changing their practices will find that the process never ends. After the first blush of novelty and enthusiasm, how can you sustain the energy, the freshness, the ideas, and most of all, the engagement of your students in learning for the love of it? Changing education, as Michael Fullan (1991) told us many years ago, "is a process, not an event" (p. 19).

Get the Support You Need

New learning about assessment is not just a nice idea; it is an essential element in changing the role and power of assessment in schools. Assessment has been neglected in teacher training and avoided in policy debates. I think it is clear that there are many thorny issues and lots to learn. Competence and confidence using classroom assessment *for* and *as* learning are not skills or dispositions that teachers will acquire by osmosis. On the other hand, there is nothing in what I'm suggesting that teachers can't understand and internalize. Unfortunately, the learning curve is fairly steep and the time is short. In the best-case scenario, policymakers, universities, school districts, principals, and teachers themselves would all have a role to play in providing the support for teachers. The more likely scenario is one where teachers and administrators will have to take charge of their own learning and lobby for what they need.

Put It All Together

Making these changes to assessment and teaching is within the purview of teachers and schools. We have seen glimpses of it in many classrooms and schools in many countries. In a 5-year study of school improvement in Manitoba, Canada (Earl & Lee, 1998), we identified a pattern in schools that were successful in making significant, whole-school changes—a pattern of activity that we have characterized as a cycle of *urgency, energy, agency,* and *more energy.* Since that time, we have added *synergy* to the mix.

Something in a school prompted a group of teachers to feel a sense of *urgency* about changing the way it did business. This urgency was experienced as a surge of *energy* that could result in productive action or a tumble into despair. When the conditions were right, these bursts of energy led to an upward spiral with an increased sense of *agency* and productivity. The *synergy* of working together moved the teachers further. This, in time, released more energy, and the cycle went on.

Schools embarked on major change initiatives when they experienced a *call to action* or critical incident that resulted in a sense of *urgency.* Something happened in these schools that jarred them and forced them to believe that change must be made, and made quickly. The staff (and sometimes the students and the community) experienced something that compelled them to action. One school coordinator describes it this way: "We had an epiphany." For others, the realization was not so dramatic—just a gnawing feeling that something was amiss. Often, this experience resulted in a challenge to how teachers viewed the world or, perhaps more precisely, their school in relation to the world. The world was not as they had known it to be, and, therefore, the status quo was no longer acceptable or appropriate. When staff came to believe that their view of the world was at odds with what they wanted to achieve, they experienced a sense of dissonance and urgency. The urgency came in many ways, but whatever the source, the staff came to see their school, themselves, and their students through different lenses.

Once schools felt the urgency to change, staff members were energized. They experienced a surge of *energy* and creativity. The energy that comes from urgency can rouse anxiety and immobilize staff when a school is not able to respond, or it can be the impetus for action. Often, teachers had to go looking for ways to make the changes that they felt were necessary. When they found support or knew that they could get it, they reported having *agency* and expressed confidence about their ability to do what they had to do, or to get the training that they needed. Sometimes, the training preceded the confidence and contributed to it, and sometimes, it was the other way around. Building capacity both internally and through professional development was critical to continued movement. Either way, the teachers experienced growth in several different areas. They increased their knowledge and skills, changed their dispositions, and established positive views about themselves and their role in changing education. Working together created *synergy* as the teachers grew in confidence and continued to extend and enhance their professional capacities. The momentum that was generated created more *energy,* and the process continued.

For me, high-quality learning for more students, more of the time, is a compelling idea that has a real urgency attached to it. I believe that assessment can be the impetus to release the energy in schools that will stimulate action. Teachers and administrators can find the resources to build capacity and create agency by working together and utilizing the synergy that results from their mutual determination and shared knowledge. And these schools can travel the tiny steps that it takes to transform education from the inside out.

> We keep asking teachers to get on luxury liners and go to places they have never been and don't believe are any better than staying at home, and we wonder why they resist. In our experience, when teachers have an image of where they want to go, they will get there, any way they can, even if it means paddling a canoe.
>
> —Earl (1999)

References

Arter, J., & McTighe, J. (2001). *Scoring rubrics in the classroom: Using performance criteria for assessing and improving student performance.* Thousand Oaks, CA: Corwin.

Assessment Reform Group. (1999). *Assessment for learning: Beyond the black box.* Cambridge, UK: University of Cambridge School of Education.

Barton, P. (1999). *Too much testing of the wrong kind, too little of the right kind in K-12 education.* Princeton, NJ: Educational Testing Service.

Beare, H. (2001). *Creating the future school.* London: Routledge/Falmer.

Biggs, J. B., & Collis, K. F. (1982). *Evaluating the quality of learning: The SOLO taxonomy.* New York: Academic Press.

Biggs, J. B., & Moore, P. J. (1993). *The process of learning* (3rd ed.). Englewood Cliffs, NJ: Prentice Hall.

Black, P. (1998). *Testing: Friend or foe? Theory and practice of assessment and testing.* London: Falmer.

Black, P., & Wiliam, D. (1998). *Inside the black box: Raising standards through classroom assessment.* London: King's College School of Education.

Bloom, B., Hastings, J., & Madaus, G. (1971). *Formative and summative evaluation of student learning.* New York: McGraw-Hill.

Brandsford, J. D., Brown, A. L., & Cocking, R. R. (1999). *How people learn: Brain, mind, experience, and school.* Washington, DC: National Academy Press.

Broadfoot, P. (1994, October). *Assessment and evaluation: To measure or to learn?* Paper presented at the International Conference on Evaluation, Toronto.

Broadfoot, P. (1996). *Education, assessment and society.* Buckingham, UK: Open University Press.

Broadfoot, P. (2001). Editorial: New wine in old bottles? The challenge of change for educational assessment. *Assessment in Education: Principles, Policy & Practice, 8*(2), 109–112.

Broadfoot, P. (2002). Assessment for lifelong learning: Challenges and choices. *Assessment in Education: Principles, Policy & Practice, 9*(1), 5–7.

Brown, R. (1989). Testing and thoughtfulness. *Educational Leadership, 46*(7), 31–33.

Clarke, S. (2001). *Unlocking formative assessment.* London: Hodder and Stoughton.

Cohen, D. K., & Hill, H. C. (2001). *Learning policy: When state education reform works.* New Haven, CT: Yale University Press.

Costa, A. (1989). Reassessing assessment. *Educational leadership, 46*(7), 2.

Costa, A. (1996). Prologue. In D. Hyerle (Ed.), *Visual tools for constructing knowledge.* Alexandria, VA: Association for Supervision and Curriculum Development.

Costa, A., & Kallick, B. (2000). *Activating and engaging habits of mind.* Alexandria, VA: Association for Supervision and Curriculum Development.

Crooks, T. (1988). The impact of classroom evaluation practices on students. *Review of Educational Research, 58*(4), 438–481.

Csikszentmihalyi, M. (1990). *Flow: The psychology of optimal experience.* New York: Harper & Row.

Cuban, L. (1984). *How teachers taught: Constancy and change in American classrooms, 1890–1980* (1st ed.). Research on Teaching Monograph Series.

Cuban, L. (1988). A fundamental puzzle of school reform. *Phi Delta Kappan, 70*(5), 341–344.

Darling-Hammond, L. (1992, November). Reframing the school reform agenda. *The School Administrator,* pp. 22–27.

Darling-Hammond, L. (1994). Performance-based assessment and educational equity. *Harvard Educational Review, 64*(1), 5–30.

Dart, B. C., Burnett, P. C., & Boulton-Lewis, G. M. (1999). Classroom learning environments and students' approaches to learning. *Learning Environments Research, 2,* 137–156.

Earl, L. (1999). *The paradox of hope: Educating young adolescents* [Monograph]. Victoria, Australia: Incorporated Association of Registered Teachers of Victoria.

Earl, L., & Cousins, J. B. (1995). *Classroom assessment: Changing the face, facing the change.* Toronto: OPSTF.

Earl, L., Fullan, M., Leithwood, K., & Watson, N. (2000). *Watching and learning: Evaluation of the implementation of the national literacy and numeracy strategies first annual report.* London: Department for Education and Employment.

Earl, L., & Katz, S. (2002). Leading schools in a data rich world. In K. Leithwood, P. Hallinger, G. C. Furman, P. Gronn, J. MacBeath, B. Mulford, & K. Riley (Eds.), *The second international handbook of educational leadership and administration.* Dordrecht, The Netherlands: Kluwer.

Earl, L., & Lee, L. (1998). *Evaluation of the Manitoba School Improvement Program.* Toronto: Walter and Duncan Gordon Foundation.

Earl, L., & LeMahieu, P. (1997). Rethinking assessment and accountability. In A. Hargreaves (Ed.), *ASCD 1997 yearbook: Rethinking educational change with heart and mind.* Alexandria, VA: Association for Supervision and Curriculum Development.

Elmore, R. (1996). Getting to scale with educational practice. *Harvard Educational Review, 66*(1), 1–25.

Ertmer, P., & Newby, T. (1996). The expert learner: Strategic, self-regulated, and reflective. *Instructional Science, 24,* 1–24.

Firestone, W. A., Mayrowetz, D., & Fairman, J. (1998). Performance-based assessment and instructional change: The effects of testing in Maine and Maryland. *Educational Evaluation and Policy Analysis, 20*(2), 95–113.

Firestone, W. A., Winter, H., & Fitz, J. (2000). Different assessments, common practice? Mathematics testing and teaching in the USA and England and Wales. *Assessment in Education: Principles, Policy & Practice, 7*(1), 13–37.

Fullan, M. (1991). *The new meaning of educational change.* Toronto: OISE Press.

Fullan, M. (2000). The return of large-scale reform. *Journal of Educational Change, 1*(2), 5–28.

Fullan, M., & Hargreaves, A. (1992). *What's worth fighting for in your school?* New York: Teachers College Press.

Gardner, H. (1991). *The unschooled mind.* New York: Basic Books.

Gipps, C. (1994). *Beyond testing: Towards a theory of educational assessment.* London: Falmer.

Gipps, C., McCallum, B., & Hargreaves, E. (2000). *What makes a good primary school teacher? Expert classroom strategies.* London: Routledge/Falmer.

Goleman, D. (1995). *Emotional intelligence: Why it can matter more than IQ.* New York: Bantam.

Gronlund, N. (2000). *How to write and use instructional objectives* (6th ed.). Englewood Cliffs, NJ: Prentice Hall.

Haertel, E. (1999). Validity arguments for high-stakes testing: In search of the evidence. *Educational Measurement: Issues and Practice, 18*(4), 5–9.

Haney, W. (Ed.). (1991). *We must take care: Fitting assessments to function.* Alexandria, VA: Association for Supervision and Curriculum Development.

Haney, W., & Madaus, G. (1989). Searching for alternatives to standardized tests: Whys, whats and whithers. *Phi Delta Kappan, 70*(9), 683–687.

Haney, W., Madaus, G., & Lyons, R. (1993). *The fractured marketplace for standardized testing.* Boston: Kluwer.

Hargreaves, A. (1994). *Changing teachers, changing times: Teachers' work and culture in the postmodern age.* London: Cassell.

Hargreaves, A., Earl, L., Moore, S., & Manning, S. (2001). *Learning to change: Teaching beyond subjects and standards.* San Francisco: Jossey-Bass.

Hargreaves, A., Earl, L., & Ryan, J. (1996). *Schooling for change: Reinventing education for early adolescents.* London: Falmer.

Hirsch, S. (2001). We're growing and changing. *Journal of Staff Development, 22*(3), 10–17.

Hyerle, D. (1996). *Visual tools.* Alexandria, VA: Association for Supervision and Curriculum Development.

Hynes, W. (1991). *The changing face of testing and assessment* [Critical Issues Report]. Arlington, VA: American Association of School Administrators.

Jensen, E. (1998). *Teaching with the brain in mind.* Alexandria, VA: Association for Supervision and Curriculum Development.

Joyce, B., & Showers, B. (1982). The coaching of teaching. *Educational Leadership, 40*(1), 4–10.

Katz, S. (1999). Substituting the symbol for the experience: Exposing a fallacy in mathematics education. *Journal of Mathematical Behavior, 17*(4), 405–410.

Katz, S., Earl, L., & Olsen, D. (2001). The paradox of classroom assessment. *McGill Journal of Education, 36*(1), 13–24.

Katz, S., Sutherland, S., & Earl, L. (in press). Developing an evaluation habit of mind. *Canadian Journal for Program Evaluation.*

Lambert, N. M., & McCombs, B. L. (1998). *How students learn: Reforming schools through learner-centered education.* Washington, DC: American Psychological Association.

Leithwood, K., Jantzi, D., & Mascall, B. (1999). *Large-scale reform: What works?* Toronto: OISE/UT.

Lemann, N. (1999). *The big test: The secret history of the American meritocracy.* New York: Farrar, Straus and Giroux.

Linn, M., & Songer, N. (1991). Cognitive and conceptual change in adolescence. *American Journal of Education, 99*(4), 379–417.

Marzano, R. (2000). *Transforming classroom grading.* Alexandria, VA: Association for Supervision and Curriculum Development.

Marzano, R., Brandt, R., Hughes, C., Jones, B., Presseisan, B., Rankin, S., & Suhor, C. (1988). *Dimensions of thinking: A framework for curriculum and instruction.* Alexandria, VA: Association for Supervision and Curriculum Development.

Marzano, R., Pickering, D., & McTighe, J. (1993). *Assessing student outcomes: Performance assessment using the Dimensions of Learning Model.* Alexandria, VA: Association for Supervision and Curriculum Development.

McDonnell, L. (1994). *Policymakers' views of student assessment.* Santa Monica, CA: RAND.

National Council of Teachers of Mathematics. (2000). *Principles and standards for school mathematics.* Reston, VA: Author.

Newmann, F. (1996). Linking restructuring to authentic student assessment. *Phi Delta Kappan, 73*(6), 458–463.

Olsen, D. R., & Bruner, J. S. (1996). Folk psychology and folk pedagogy. In D. R. Olsen & N. Torrance (Eds.), *The handbook of education and human development.* Cambridge, MA: Basil Blackwell.

Perkins, D. (1992). *Smart schools: From training memories to educating minds.* New York: Free Press.

Perkins, D., & Unger, C. (Eds.). (2000). *Teaching and learning for understanding.* Mahwah, NJ: Lawrence Erlbaum.

Pollard, A., & Filer, A. (1999). *The social world of children's learning.* London: Cassell.

Popham, J. (1995). *Classroom assessment: What teachers need to know.* Boston: Allyn & Bacon.

Popham, J. (2002). Right task, wrong tool. *American School Board Journal, 189*(2), 18–22.

Rogers, T. (1991). Educational assessment in Canada. *Alberta Journal of Educational Research, 36*(2), 179–192.

Sadler, R. (1989). Formative assessment and the design of instructional systems. *Instructional Science, 18,* 119–144.

Sarason, S. (1996). *Revisiting "The culture of school and the problem of change."* New York: Teachers College Press.

Senge, P. (1990). *The fifth discipline: The art and practice of the learning organization.* New York: Doubleday.

Shepard, L. (1989). Why we need better assessments. *Educational Leadership,* *46*(7), 4–9.

Shepard, L. (2000, April). *The role of assessment in a learning culture: Presidential address.* Paper presented at the annual meeting of the American Education Research Association, New Orleans.

Stevenson, H., & Stigler, J. (1992). *The learning gap: Why our schools are failing and what we can learn from Japanese and Chinese education.* New York: Summit.

Stiggins, R. (1990). Toward a relevant classroom assessment research agenda. *Alberta Journal of Educational Research, 36*(1), 92–97.

Stiggins, R. (1991). Assessment literacy. *Phi Delta Kappan, 72*(7), 534–539.

Stiggins, R. (1993, May). *Student-centered assessment.* Paper presented at the workshop sponsored by the Association of Educational Research Officers of Toronto.

Stiggins, R. (1994). *Student-centered classroom assessment.* New York: Merrill.

Stiggins, R. (1997). *Student-centered classroom assessment* (2nd ed.). Upper Saddle River, NJ: Prentice Hall.

Stiggins, R. (2001). *Student-involved classroom assessment* (3rd ed.). Upper Saddle River, NJ: Prentice Hall.

Stoll, L., Fink, D., & Earl, L. (2002). *It's about learning (and it's about time): What's in it for schools?* London: Routledge Falmer.

Sutton, R. (1995). *Assessment for learning.* Salford, UK: RS Publications.

Torrance, H. (2001). Assessment for learning: Developing formative assessment in the classroom. *Professional Journal for Primary Education, 29*(3), 26–32.

Torrance, H., & Pryor, J. (1998). *Investigating formative assessment.* Buckingham, UK: Open University Press.

Vygotsky, L. S. (1978). *Mind in society: The development of the higher psychological processes.* Cambridge, MA: Harvard University Press. (Originally published 1930)

Watkins, C., Carnell, E., Lodge, C., Wagner, P., & Whalley, C. (2001). *Learning about learning: Staff development resources from NAPCE.* Unpublished manuscript, London.

Weinstein, R. S. (1998). Promoting positive expectations in schooling. In N. M. Lambert & B. L. McCombs (Eds.), *How students learn: Reforming schools through learner-centered education.* Washington, DC: American Psychological Association.

Wenglinsky, J. (2002). How schools matter: The link between teacher and classroom practices and student academic performance. *Education Policy Analysis Archives, 10*(12), 1–28.

Whitty, G., Power, S., & Halpin, D. (1998). *Devolution and choice in education: The school, the state, the market.* Buckingham, UK: Open University Press.

Wiggins, G. (1989). Teaching to the (authentic) test. *Educational Leadership, 46*(7), 41–47.

Wiggins, G. (1993). *Assessing student performance.* San Francisco: Jossey-Bass.

Wiggins, G. (1998). *Educative assessment: Designing assessments to inform and improve performance.* San Francisco: Jossey-Bass.

Wiggins, G., & McTighe, J. (1999). *Understanding by design.* Alexandria, VA: Association for Supervision and Curriculum Development.

Wilson, R. (1994, May). *Back to basics: A revisionist model of classroom-based assessment.* Paper presented at the Canadian Educational Research Association, Calgary, AB.

Wilson, R. (1996). *Assessing students in classrooms and schools.* Scarborough, UK: Allyn & Bacon.

Wolf, D., Bixby, J., Glenn, J., & Gardner, H. (1991). To use their minds well: Investigating new forms of student assessment. *Review of Research in Education, 17,* 31–74.

Young, S., & Wilson, R. (2000). *Assessment and learning: The ICE approach.* Winnipeg, MB: Portage & Main Press.

Zmuda, A., & Tomaino, M. (2001). *The competent classroom: Aligning high school curriculum, standards, and assessment—A creative teaching guide.* Washington, DC: National Education Association.

Index

**CORWIN
PRESS**

The Corwin Press logo—a raven striding across an open book—represents the happy union of courage and learning. We are a professional-level publisher of books and journals for K-12 educators, and we are committed to creating and providing resources that embody these qualities. Corwin's motto is "Success for All Learners."

Printed in the United States
135942LV00002B/7/P